SPARKLING WINE

The Vineyards of England and Wales

ACC ART BOOKS

CONTENTS

HOW TO USE THIS BOOK

....

This book is a celebration of English and Welsh sparkling wines and the vineyards that produce them. Each vineyard has a story to tell and features to note. For every vineyard in the book, there are details on the terroir, the blend of available sparkling wines and, where advised, the winemaker. Where a vineyard has more than one plot or location, it is the initial plot that is described in detail. Practical information on opening times, tours, contact details and buying options is also included.

The vineyards included represent a selection of those in England and Wales currently producing sparkling wine; the sites are sprinkled across the counties of southern, central and northern England, and parts of Wales, to provide insight into the wonderful breadth of sparkling wines available. There are, of course, many other English and Welsh vineyards producing sparkling wines that are not included here.

For the wine listings at each vineyard, details of classification, sweetness, grape variety and vintage are included where available:

Classification

'English wine' is the generic title given to all wine produced anywhere in the UK from grapes sourced entirely within the UK. It now has its own classification system:

** Protected Designation of Origin (PDO). The grapes used in the production of PDO wine must be drawn from the designated PDO area and are only of the *Vitis vinifera* genus. The production of the wine also takes place in the named area ('area' being the county within which the vineyard lies and the directly adjoining counties).

* Protected Geographical Indication (PGI). The wine possesses a specific quality, reputation or other characteristics attributable to the geographical region (England and Wales are defined as individual 'regions'). At least 85 per cent of the grapes used in the production a PGI wine will have come from that area and are of the *Vitis vinifera* genus or a cross of *Vitis vinifera* and another genus of *Vitis*. The wine will also be produced within the same, named geographical region.

Sweetness

(1 – 7) Where offered by the vineyard, the nominal sweetness of a wine is indicated according to the recognised scale of 1 to 7 for sparkling wine (1 being the driest).

Alcohol

% The alcohol content of each sparkling wine is given as a percentage, and, where known, followed by the dosage.

Dosage

Where available, the residual sugar content – dosage – is given for each wine in grams per litre (g/lt). The dosage gives an indication to the style of sparkling wine:

<6 g/lt – extra brut
<12 g/lt – brut
12 to 17 g/lt – extra dry
17 to 32 g/lt – sec
32 to 50 g/lt – demi-sec
>50 – doux

NV Where a sparkling wine is designated 'NV' (non-vintage) it has been made to a consistent style and taste, even while the proportion of the grape varieties used or blended may vary from year to year depending upon the sweetness of the grape juice.

Where a wine is made solely from a designated year's crop (vintage), the proportion of grape varieties in the blend will be exclusive to that year. Sometimes, the grapes may come exclusively from one designated plot or vineyard and will be stated as such.

The vagaries of the British climate mean that many vineyards will, from year to year, completely change the grape varieties used in the blending of a wine to maintain a similar or identical style and taste throughout, whilst keeping the same label or name. The alcoholic strength of the wine may also vary.

All the sparkling wines in this book have been produced using the 'traditional method' (the *méthode champenoise*).

All of the vineyards listed have gained awards for their sparkling wines at regional or national level. However, those listed with the awarding body have gained these international trophies in the recent past.

Stewart Wilde

INTRODUCTION

England and Wales are geographically marginal for growing wine grapes. However, the nature of this island, with its geology, climate and landscape, has created pockets of land that are, with their peculiar microclimates, eminently suitable for viticulture. Indeed, it's their marginality and diversity that give English and Welsh wines – sparkling wines in particular – their own special character. Encouraged by changes in climate and an upsurge in producers, a few of these pockets are producing wines of such exceptional quality that they are challenging the recognised premier wines of the world in competitions for best in class, outshining the likes of Champagne on the international stage.

Whilst global acclaim for English and Welsh sparkling wines is a recent phenomenon, the region has cultivated vines for millennia. The Romans introduced viticulture, planting vines adjacent to their camps. After the Romans came monastic communities, producing wine for their own consumption, and then came the grand houses of the Crown and aristocracy. During this latter period, in 1662, Dr Christopher Merrett, an English scientist, presented a paper to the Royal Society describing the making of sparkling wine, predating the better-known Dom Pérignon by some thirty years. The later seventeenth century also saw the development of the thicker glass required to withstand the air pressure generated by Merret's process. And yet, despite Merret's work and the proliferation of small-scale winemakers, indigenous winemaking went into decline, the causes being more political than climatic.

It took a handful of enthusiastic, often eccentric, individuals to reinvent winemaking in England and Wales after the Second World War. They took small patches of land and began producing still wines from 'cool climate' grapes. As the development of sparkling wine emerged, the wines began to grow in quality. When growers began planting classic champagne varieties, often dedicating their production solely to sparkling wines, this side of the industry flourished. Often, they acquired their expertise with the help of Plumpton College (see page 77), one of the primary viticultural education establishments in the world, and from the best wine producers elsewhere, but maintained the small-scale, artisanal approach of the owner/maker.

Of the 600 plus vineyards in England and Wales today, fewer than 100 have ten acres or more of vines. Production is often small scale, labour intensive and time consuming and, consequently, the resulting sparkling wine can appear expensive to the consumer. However, the small scale creates sparkling wines with distinct individual styles. For example, the initial juice may be low-pressure cylindrical or basket pressed and the base wines may be vinified in wood, concrete or stainless steel. All such permutations impart individual characteristics to the finished sparkling wine.

This book will guide you to a selection of English and Welsh vineyards, to the producers and their celebrated sparkling wines. Several are off the beaten track, some are remote, many reside in areas of outstanding natural beauty. You can even arrive at one by boat. Some have accommodation, allowing for a longer visit. In common, the vineyards and their owners share an infectious passion for the new era of English and Welsh sparkling wine; there's never been a better time to pay them a visit.

SPARKLING WINE GRAPE VARIETIES

Champagne grape varieties

WHITE

Chardonnay
A fruitful, thin-skinned, alcoholic and complex grape variety with slight sweetness when barrel fermented. Always shows signs of the local terroir on the palate. When picked not fully ripe has crisp acidity. The most universally used white grape variety for sparkling wine.

Petit Meslier
A little-known grape variety with only a small planting. Low yielding but quite fruity.

Pinot Blanc
An easy-ripening, low-yielding grape variety with high acidity giving a full-bodied crisp and dry finish.

Pinot Gris
A late-ripening, slightly perfumed grape variety with low acidity, evident residual sugar and dry, delicate and flavoursome finish.

RED

Pinot Meunier
An early-ripening grape variety with good acidity and relatively high alcohol level. It has youthful fruitiness and gives a characterful finish.

Pinot Noir
An unpredictable, early-ripening grape variety with an unreliable yield and an ability to highlight the local terroir. It is thin skinned and has low tannin levels with a sweet fruitiness but can also be quite vegetal. Late picking can limit the aroma and acidity.

Non-champagne grape varieties

WHITE

Auxerrois
A late-ripening grape variety that has floral and fruit scents and lower acidity. Responds well to a light amount of oak and is principally used in a blend.

Bacchus
Reminiscent of a New World Sauvignon Blanc for grassiness and dry aromas but with more grapey fruit on the palate and softer, low and crisp acidity. An early- ripening grape variety.

Huxelrebe	Muscat flavour and fruity with good sugar and acidity levels. Blends to give weight.
Madeleine Angevine	An early-ripening grape variety with positive aroma and crisp acidity.
Müller-Thurgau	An early-ripening aromatic grape variety with perceptible fruit flavours and low acidity. Gives plentiful amounts of fruit which has a slight sweetness.
Orion	An aromatic and fruity grape variety with soft acidity. Provides a crisp finish.
Phoenix	A high-yielding herbaceous and aromatic grape variety with higher sugar and lower acidity. Can produce a full-bodied wine.
Reichensteiner	An early-ripening grape variety with higher natural sugar and lower acidity. Capable of producing a full-bodied wine.
Scheurebe	A late-ripening fruity and herbaceous grape variety producing racy flavours and rich acidity.
Schönburger	A grape variety that is susceptible to low acidity levels, producing light and fruity wines. High in residual sugars; can produce a full-bodied wine.
Seyval Blanc	A late-ripening grape variety with low natural sugar and higher acidity levels together with a grassy herbaceousness. Picks up and highlights the local terroir.

RED

Cabernet Cortis	A newly developed hybrid grape variety with only a small planting and very little experience, having only produced rosé wine to date. Barrel aging can enhance the resulting flavours.
Dornfelder	An aromatic and floral grape variety with good acidity and occasional sweetness.
Gamay	An early-ripening aromatic grape variety with higher acidity and producing a lower alcohol level. Also with very light tannins.
Pinot Noir Précoce	An early-ripening, low-yielding grape variety.
Rondo	An early-ripening, good-cropping grape variety with good fruit and acidity. Capable of producing a full-bodied wine.
Triomphe	An early-ripening grape variety whose taste can be described as 'foxy'.

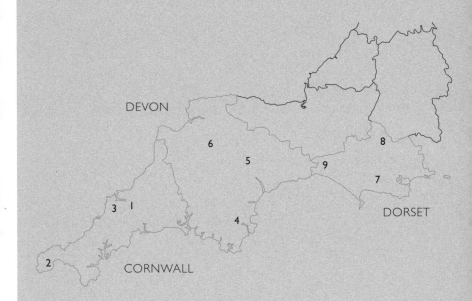

DEVON

CORNWALL

DORSET

1. SOUTH WEST

CORNWALL
1. Camel Valley
2. Polgoon
3. Trevibban Mill

DEVON
4. Sharpham
5. Yearlstone
6. Ten Acres

DORSET
7. Langham Wine Estate
8. Melbury Vale
9. Furleigh Estate

CAMEL VALLEY

Little Denby Farm, Nanstallon,
Bodmin, PL30 5LG
01208 77959
camelvalley.com

24.50 acres (approx. 1400 vines/acre)
First planted in 1988
Total wine production: 100,000
bottles annually
Winemaker: Sam Lindo

Terroir
Between 18m and 55m above sea level
South-facing slope
Medium loam over ancient slate

Visiting and buying
Open all year, Mon to Fri, 10am to 5pm;
Easter to Oct, Sat, 10am to 5pm; guided
tour, April to Sept, Mon to Fri, 2.30pm; April
to Oct, Weds, 5pm (groups only by prior
arrangement). Self-catering cottages at
vineyard. 'Wine by the glass' vouchers
available online. Wine sales at cellar door,
by mail order, online and at selected
national and local stockists.

In 1989, Bob and Annie Lindo planted 8000
vines on the steeply sloping valley side of
the Camel River, putting down roots on a
former sheep and cattle farm. Today, the
vineyard, powered entirely by self-generated
solar energy, boasts 32,000 vines and a
Royal Warrant for its sparkling wine.

Bob and Annie learned their craft by
reading about the subject, attending various
courses and visiting overseas vineyards, to
become accredited winemakers for the
Camel Valley vineyard. Several awards later,
Bob has now handed over the winemaking
responsibilities to his son, Sam, who has
taken the vineyard, and its wines, to new
heights. Sam has won regional, national and
international medals and trophies, and been
named UK Winemaker of the Year on three
occasions. Annie continues as a winemaker
at Camel Valley, still tending her own
field, single-handed, to produce 'Annie's
Anniversary' sparkling wine. Bob, as a vocal
supporter of English and Welsh wines,
and Cornish wines in particular, has been
featured with the vineyard and its wines on
radio and TV on several occasions. In 2017,
the vineyard was recognised as the 'Best
Run Sustainable Cornish Business'. Camel
Valley is also the only English vineyard with
a Royal Warrant, by appointment to HRH
the Prince of Wales.

All the sparkling wines at Camel Valley are
produced in the winery at the vineyard
and are a combination of champagne and
non-champagne grapes. The vineyard also
produces white, rosé and red still wines
and a sparkling cider.

Cornwall

WHITE

* (2) Cornwall – 2014
12.5% – (9.0 g/lt)
Brut
*English hedgerow aromas and touch of
honey with refined fruit*
Chardonnay (40%), Seyval Blanc (35%),
Pinot Noir (25%)

** (2) Annie's Anniversary – 2014
12.5% – (10.0 g/lt)
Brut
*Zippily fresh, lemony and tropical with
yeastier depths*
Seyval Blanc (100%)

** (1) Chardonnay – 2014
12.5% – (10.0 g/lt)
Brut
*Fruity nose with buttered pastry and creamy
texture*
Chardonnay (100%)

** (2) White Pinot Noir – 2014
12.0% – (10.5 g/lt)
Brut
*Lemon zest and peach with fine biscuity
complexity*
Pinot Noir (100%)

ROSÉ

Rosé Brut – 2016
12.5% – (12.0 g/lt)
*Strawberry and raspberry with refreshing
and balanced acidity*
Pinot Noir (100%)

(2) Raymond Blanc de Noir – 2015
11.5% – (9.0 g/lt)
Brut
*Red fruit flavours with hints of toasty
caramel and vanilla*
Pinot Noir (100%)

RED

Sparkling Red – 2015
12.5% – (12.0 g/lt)
Brut
Cranberry and redcurrant
Rondo (100%)

POLGOON

Rosehill, Penzance, TR20 8TE
01736 333946
polgoon.com

13 acres (approx. 1000 vines/acre)
First planted in 2003
Total wine production: 25,000 to 30,000
bottles annually
Winemaker: John Coulson

Terroir
Approx. 30m above sea level
South-facing slopes
Well-drained sandy loam

Visiting and buying
April to Dec, Mon to Sat, 9am to 5.30pm,
Sun, 10.30am to 4pm; Jan and Feb,
Mon to Sat only, 9am to 3pm (groups
only by prior arrangement); guided tour,
April to Sept, Weds, Thurs, Fri, 2pm.
Three-bedroom cottage at vineyard.
Wine sales at cellar door, online and at
selected stockists.

In 2003, John and Kim Coulson made a dramatic life change. After several years working as fish merchants, they decided to go into wine production, convinced that they could produce artisan wines as a family operation on the farm they had just bought. Half the farm was given over to vines and their first vintage, a still rosé, was a medal winner in a national competition. Initially planted on open ground, but now part-planted in polytunnels, the vineyard has grown steadily over the years.

Polgoon's sparkling wines are produced from a combination of recognised champagne and non-champagne grapes. These grapes are now vinified on site in the newly built winery. John, the winemaker, has qualified for the role through years of hands-on experience. White, rosé and red still wines, fruit drinks and ciders are also produced at the vineyard.

WHITE

Sparkling Seyval Blanc – 2014
12.0% – (10.0 g/lt)
Brut
Granny Smith apple with pear, lemongrass and youthful acidity
Seyval Blanc (100%)

ROSÉ

Sparkling Rosé – 2014
12.0% – (8.7 g/lt)
Dry
Ripe berry flavours with raspberry, strawberry and crisp finish
Pinot Noir (100%)

TREVIBBAN MILL

Dark Lane, Wadebridge,
Nr Padstow, PL27 7SE
01841 541413
trevibbanmill.com

7.5 acres (approx. 1300 vines/acre)
First planted in 2008
Total wine production: 22,000
bottles annually
Winemaker: Manuel Kowalewski

Terroir
Between 60m and 90m above sea level
South-facing slope
Easy-draining poor slatey soil

Visiting and buying
Open all year, Weds to Sun, 12noon to
5pm (groups only by prior arrangement);
guided tour, Weds and Thurs, 5pm.
Restaurant and Eco Lodge at vineyard.
Wine sales at cellar door and online.

What started off for Engin and Liz Mumcuoglu as a restoration project on an eighteenth-century flour mill grew to include a vineyard, planted on the surrounding land. Over time Trevibban has developed into a fully integrated organic and energy-efficient production unit. The winery is newly built and solar fuelled with event facilities and a refreshment area that overlooks an attractive flower garden, the vineyard and the beautiful St Issey valley in which it is situated.

Trevibban Mill's sparkling wines are made from champagne and non-champagne grapes and give the wine a distinctive English flavour. The vineyard also produces white, rosé and red still wine together with sparkling and still cider.

WHITE

(1) Blanc de Blancs – 2014
12.0% – (<1.0 g/lt)
Dry
Complex flavours
Chardonnay (100%)

ROSÉ

(1) Sparkling Pink – 2014
12.5% – (2.6 g/lt)
Brut
Blackberry, sour cherry and plum with fresh acidity
Dornfelder (100%)

SHARPHAM

Sharpham Estate, Ashprington,
Totnes, TQ9 7UT
01803 732203
sharpham.com

10 acres (approx. 1000 vines/acre)
First planted in 1981
Total wine production: approx. 40,000
bottles annually
Winemakers: Duncan Schwab
and Tommy Grimshaw

Terroir
Between 30m and 50m above sea level
South-east facing slope
Silty clay loam sandstone soil

Visiting and buying
March, Mon to Sat, 10am to 5pm; April
to Oct, daily 10am to 5pm; Nov, Mon to
Sat, 10am to 3pm (groups only by prior
arrangement); self-guided walkabout
(when open); tutored tastings, daily (when
open). Wine sales at cellar door, online
and at local stockists.

Sharpham is situated on the sheltered, southerly facing, steeply sloping banks of the River Dart. Although planted by Maurice Ash in 1981, the vineyard, with its own moorings for any arrival by water, is part of a much larger thousand-year-old estate – within which lies a particularly large water meadow. The vineyard benefits from a particular soil structure and microclimate that enable it to produce grapes of the highest quality.

Sharpham's sparkling wines have consistently won awards and medals at regional, national and international competitions. The sparkling wines are made of permitted home-grown – and occasionally bought-in – champagne grapes that are vinified in the onsite winery and then matured and stored elsewhere. The vineyard also produces white, rosé and red still wines as well as renowned cheeses.

WHITE

** (2) Sparkling Blanc – 2014
12.0% – (11.4 g/lt)
Brut
Crisp initial palate with light biscuity notes and long, dry finish
Pinot Noir (57%), Chardonnay (33%), Pinot Meunier (10%)

** (2) Sparkling Reserve – NV
12.0% – (12.0 g/lt)
Brut
Flavours of almonds with upfront ripe dragon fruit
Pinot Noir, Pinot Blanc, Chardonnay

ROSÉ

* (2) Sparkling Pink – 2014
12.0% – (9.4 g/lt)
Brut
Strawberry palate with refreshing citrus overtones
Chardonnay (50%), Pinot Noir (45%), Pinot Meunier (5%)

YEARLSTONE

Bickleigh, Tiverton, EX16 8RL
01884 855700
yearlstone.co.uk

7.5 acres (approx. 1200 vines/acre)
First planted in 1976
Total wine production: approx. 70,000
bottles annually
Winemaker: Juliet White

Terroir
Between 37m and 76m above sea level
South and south-west facing slopes
Red clay-loam soil over sandstone

Visiting and buying
Open by appointment only. Guided tours by
prior arrangement. Wine sales at cellar door,
online, by mail order and at local stockists.

Devon's oldest vineyard was originally
planted in 1976 by Gillian Peakes, a
prominent member of the post-war English
planting fraternity. The present owners took
over when Gillian died, extending the area
under vine to its present size. The vineyard
is situated at the top of a steep southerly
facing slope overlooking the River Exe. The
vines are widely spaced and – unusually –
face east/west, to get the most from what
is a marginal climate for ripening grapes.
Facing east/west also reduces the likelihood
of mildew developing from the early
morning mists that roll along the valley floor.

The sparkling wines produced in the winery
at Yearlstone are sometimes supplemented
by grapes from other local vineyards, of both
champagne and non-champagne varieties.
The vineyard has won a number of regional
and national awards and medals, and the
present owner and winemaker, Juliet White,
also makes wines for other local vineyards.

WHITE

Vintage Brut – 2013
12.0% – (8.0 g/lt)
Yeasty with green apple
Pinot Noir (50%), Seyval Blanc (50%)

ROSÉ

Vintage Brut Rosé – 2013
12.0% – (10.0 g/lt)
Yeasty with red fruit
Pinot Noir (100%)

TEN ACRES

Torrington Road, Winkleigh, EX19 8EY
01837 83892
tenacresvineyardcamping.co.uk

2.5 acres (approx. 1000 vines/acre)
First planted in 2008
Total wine production: between 2000 and
10,000 bottles annually
Winemaker: Toby McKinnel

Terroir
Approx. 150m above sea level
South-facing slope
Loam over schisty slate soils

Visiting and buying
May to Sept, Tues and Thurs, 10am to 8pm,
Weds, 5pm to 8pm; or by appointment
(groups only by prior arrangement); self-
guided walkabout (when open); guided tour,
Sat, 5pm. Campsite at vineyard. Wine sales
at cellar door and farmers' markets.

Planted in 2008 by Toby and Esther
McKinnel on their return to Britain after
living overseas, this boutique vineyard is
situated half a mile down a quiet country
track, on the south-facing slope of what
used to be Winkleigh wartime airfield.

Toby and Esther run the vineyard alongside
their campsite, and its wines are produced
principally for those staying at the location
– although they can be bought by anyone
visiting the cellar door. The sparkling wine,
produced from non-champagne grapes, is
made inhouse in the compact winery. The
vineyard also produces white and rosé
still wines and has a red wine vinified at a
nearby winery.

WHITE

Goldfinch – NV
11.5% – (6.0 g/lt)
Brut
Fruity with soft acidity
Seyval Blanc, Orion

LANGHAM WINE ESTATE

Crawthorne, Dewlish,
Dorchester, DT2 7NG
01258 839095
langhamwine.co.uk

30 acres (approx. 1000 vines/acre)
First planted in 2009
Total wine production: approx. 5000
bottles annually
Winemaker: Daniel Ham

Terroir
Approx. 90m above sea level
South-facing slope
Sandy-loam soils over Jurassic chalk

Visiting and buying
Jan and Feb, Thurs to Sat, 10am to 4pm;
March to Dec, Weds to Sat, 10am to 4pm;
at other times by appointment only (groups
only by prior arrangement); guided tours by
appointment. Wine sales at cellar door,
online and at selected national stockists.

When John Langham bought the Grade 1
listed Melcombe Manor, a large farming
estate of around 2500 acres dating to the
time of Edward VI, he planted a small, token
vineyard. In 2009, his son Justin developed the
vineyard into a commercial venture, taking
advantage of the site's unique microclimate.
The former milking parlour now forms the
present-day winery, where the award and
medal-winning sparkling wines are produced
from home-grown Champagne grapes.

WHITE

(2) Classic Cuvée – 2014
12.0% – (10.0 g/lt)
Oaked/Brut
Summer fruit with hint of peach and acidic
backbone
Chardonnay (50%), Pinot Noir (25%),
Pinot Meunier (25%)

(1) Blanc de Blancs – 2014
12.5% – (10.0 g/lt)
Brut/Aromatic
Lemon peel with enveloping brioche overlay
Chardonnay (100%)

(2) Blanc de Noirs – 2013
12.0% – (10.0 g/lt)
Brut
Red fruit, violets and brioche aromas with
citrus fruit
Pinot Noir (58%), Pinot Meunier (42%)

ROSÉ

Rosé – 2014
12.5% – (10.5 g/lt)
Brut
Buttery with red cherry flavours and herby
character
Pinot Noir (89%), Chardonnay (11%)

MELBURY VALE

Foots Hill, Cann, SP7 0BW
01747 854206
mvwinery.co.uk

2 acres (approx. 1000 vines/acre)
First planted in 2006
Total wine production: approx. 25,000
bottles annually
Winemaker: Joseph Pestell

Terroir
Approx. 150m above sea level
South-facing slopes
Clay soils

Visiting and buying
Open all year, Fri and Sat, 11.30am to 6pm;
Dec, also Sun, 10am to 4pm (groups only by
prior arrangement); guided tours, Feb to Sept,
Fri and Sat, 11.30am. Self-catering cottage
at vineyard. Wine sales at cellar door, farm
shows and selected local stockists.

Originally bought by a brother and sister,
Glyn and Clare Pestell, as a derelict
and dilapidated twenty-eight-acre farm,
Melbury Vale has since been developed
into a multi-family working vineyard.
This two-acre vineyard is situated on the
south-facing hillside of the Stirkel Valley at
Cann Bridge. The newly built winery has
been an important part of this progression;
the sustainable building features a flower
meadow on the roof and a rainwater-
harvesting system.

The sparkling wines at Melbury Vale are a
blend of one champagne grape variety and
other dominant non-champagne varieties.
This blending gives the wines what has been
described as an 'English style'. In the summer
months they serve afternoon tea, enjoyed on
a Saturday in the company of the winemaker
no less. The vineyard also produces white,
rosé and red still wines, cider, grape-wine
brandy, fusions and fruit liqueurs.

WHITE

(2) Grace – NV
12.0% – (11.99 g/lt)
Brut
Lively and fragrant nose
Seyval Blanc, Reichensteiner and others

ROSÉ

(2) Decadence – NV
12.0% – (11.99 g/lt)
Brut
Fruity nose with strawberry and elderflower notes
Seyval Blanc, Pinot Noir

FURLEIGH ESTATE

Salway Ash, Bridport, DT6 5JF
01308 488991
furleighestate.co.uk

40 acres (approx. 1300 vines/acre)
First planted in 2005
Total wine production: approx. 50,000
bottles annually
Winemaker: Ian Edwards

Terroir
Approx. 100m above sea level
South-facing slope
Sandy-loam soils

Visiting and buying
Open all year, Mon to Sat, 11am to
5pm; at other times by appointment
only (groups only by prior arrangement);
guided tours all year, Fri and Sat, 11am
and 2.30pm. Wine sales at cellar door,
online, in farm shops and selected
national stockists.

Furleigh Estate is situated in the bucolic Dorset countryside, close to the Jurassic Coast where the fossil-encrusted soil is ideal for vine cultivation. The former dairy farm was Rebecca Hansford's childhood home. When she and her husband purchased the farm themselves in 2005 they began converting it into a vineyard.

The sparkling wines at Furleigh, made from champagne grapes by the owner and winemaker Ian Edwards, have won several national and international awards and medals during the vineyard's relatively short life. Guided tours and tastings take place on the hoof, with the wines sampled as visitors walk around the vineyard and winery. The vineyard also produces white, pink and red still wines.

WHITE

(2) Classic Cuvée – 2014
12.0% – (14.0 g/lt)
Extra sec
Citrus fruit with grapefruit and lemon
Chardonnay (40%), Pinot Noir (30%), Pinot Meunier (30%)

(2) Blanc de Noirs – 2014
12.0% – (10.3 g/lt)
Off dry/Brut
Green fruits, nettle with rich ripe fruit flavours
Pinot Noir (88%), Pinot Meunier (12%)

(1) Blanc de Blancs – 2013
12.0% – (6.4 g/lt)
Brut
Acacia and elderflower with lemon, grapefruit and minerality
Chardonnay (100%)

ROSÉ

Rosé – NV
12.0% – (8.3 g/lt)
Brut
Strawberry and white cherries with red berries and soft minerality
Pinot Noir, Chardonnay, Pinot Meunier

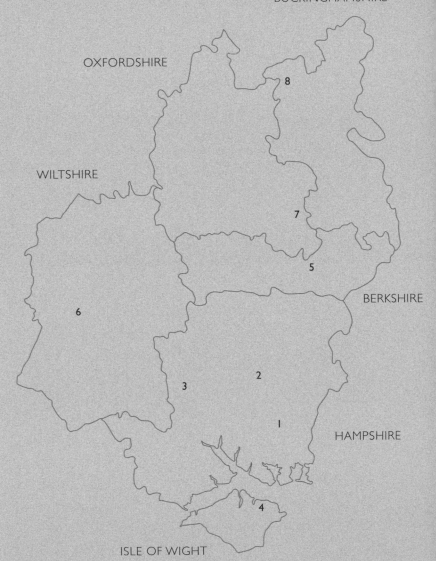

BUCKINGHAMSHIRE

OXFORDSHIRE

WILTSHIRE

BERKSHIRE

HAMPSHIRE

ISLE OF WIGHT

8

7

5

6

3

2

1

4

2. SOUTH CENTRAL

HAMPSHIRE
1. Hambledon
2. Hattingley Valley
3. Cottonworth

ISLE OF WIGHT
4. Rosemary

BERKSHIRE
5. Stanlake Park

WILTSHIRE
6. a'Beckett's

OXFORDSHIRE
7. Chiltern Valley

BUCKINGHAMSHIRE
8. Chafor Estate

HAMBLEDON

The Vineyard, East Street,
Hambledon, PO7 4RY
02392 632358
hambledonvineyard.co.uk

240 acres (approx. 2000 vines/acre)
First planted in 1952
Total wine production: approx. 140,000
bottles annually
Winemaker: Felix Gabillet

Terroir
Between 50m and 100m above sea level
South-facing slopes
Sedimentary limestone over chalky soils

Visiting and buying
Open all year, Mon to Fri, 9am to 5pm;
groups by prior arrangement only; guided
tours, Tues, Thurs and Sat, 2pm. Wine sales at
cellar door, online and at selected local and
national stockists.

When Sir Guy Salisbury-Jones planted
vines at Hambledon in 1952, he created
the first of a new post-war generation of
English and Welsh vineyards. He did so,
incidentally, in the same village that saw the
birth of modern cricket (when someone
added a third stump at either end of the
pitch in the 1770s).

Hambledon has played an important role
in the development of English and Welsh
wine. In its early years, the vineyard's
sparkling wine was regularly served at
prestige events and venues, not least on
board the *QE2* and at various British
embassies.

Reborn and rejuvenated over the last two
decades, under the guidance of the newest
owner Ian Kellett, today Hambledon
exports its sparkling wine around the
world and has re-established its position as
a prestige brand. Recognised, home-grown
champagne grapes are used in all of the
sparkling wines.

WHITE

** (1) Classic Cuvée – NV
12.0% – (7.0 g/lt)
Brut
Hint of smoke on greengage, red plum and
dessert apples
Chardonnay, Pinot Meunier, Pinot Noir

** (2) Premiere Cuvée – NV
12.0% – (8.0 g/lt)
Brut
Seville orange and brioche with dried apricots,
citrus and vanilla
Chardonnay, Pinot Noir, Pinot Meunier

HATTINGLEY VALLEY

Wield Yard, Lower Wield,
Alresford, SO24 9AJ
01256 389188
hattingleyvalley.co.uk

60 acres (approx. 2000 vines/acre)
First planted in 2008
Total wine production: approx. 200,000
bottles annually
Winemakers: Emma Rice

Terroir
Approx. 187m above sea level
South facing
Chalky bedrock

Visiting and buying
Open all year, Mon to Sat, 9am to 6pm;
groups by prior arrangement only; guided
tours, April to Sept, first Sat of each month.
Wine sales at cellar door and selected
national stockists.

The owners of Hattingley Valley believe
it to be the largest contracted producer
of sparkling wine in the UK. They make
sparkling wines from champagne and
non-champagne grapes; the fruit used for
its own-label wines is taken both from
Hattingley's own vineyards and those of
other local growers.

The sparkling wines at Hattingley
have received many regional, national
and international awards and medals.
The owners, and their internationally
recognised winemakers, are rightly proud
of their achievements, particularly given
the short time period that has elapsed
since the vines were planted in 2008,
and the traditionally long maturation
time for sparkling wine. Solar energy is
comprehensively used at the vineyard for
as many purposes as possible. Hattingley
also produces a still dessert wine.

WHITE

** (2) Blanc de Blancs – 2011
12.0% – (10.0 g/lt)
Oaked/Brut
White fruit, toasty and honeyed with ripe apple and soft acidity
Chardonnay (100%)

** (2) Classic Reserve – NV
12.0% – (7.0 g/lt)
Oaked/Brut
Hedgerow flowers with green fruit and toasty flavour
Chardonnay, Pinot Noir, Pinot Meunier, Pinot Gris

(1) Kings Cuvée – 2013
12.0% – (5.0 g/lt)
Oaked/Brut
Approachable fruit, creamy
Chardonnay (70%), Pinot Noir (30%)

(4) Demi-Sec – 2013
11.0% – (38.0 g/lt)
Oaked/Brut
Apple and blackberry aromas with ripe red fruit and pastries
Pinot Noir (59%), Pinot Meunier (36%), Pinot Noir Précoce (5%)

ROSÉ

** (2) Rosé – 2014
12.0% – (8.0 g/lt)
Oaked/Full bod./Brut
Red fruit and fresh acidity with toasty notes
Pinot Noir (60%), Pinot Meunier (38%), Pinot Noir Précoce (2%)

RED

(1) Sparkling Red Pinot – 2015
12.0% – (5.0 g/lt)
Oaked/Brut
Red cherries, raspberries and strawberries and cream
Pinot Noir (83%), Pinot Noir Précoce (17%)

COTTONWORTH

Fullerton Farms, Fullerton Road,
Cottonworth, SP11 7JX
01264 860531
cottonworth.co.uk

30 acres (approx. 1500 vines/acre)
First planted in 2005
Total wine production: approx. 10,000
bottles annually
Winemakers: Emma Rice

Terroir
Between 40m and 70m above sea level
South-facing slopes
Chalky soils

Visiting and buying
Open all year, Thurs to Sat, 10am to
4pm; by appointment only at other
times; guided tours, June to Oct, Fri and
Sat, 12noon. Wine sales at cellar door,
online and at local stockists.

Hugh Liddell, the original winemaker on the family farm, first produced a still rosé in 2008. A later planting of the classic champagne grapes took the vineyard into sparkling wines.

The vines at Cottonworth benefit greatly from the particular microclimate of the Test Valley in which they lie. South-west to south-east slopes, a drying prevailing wind (helping to prevent disease) and chalky soils collaborate to produce first-class, award-winning sparkling wines. Indeed, today the vineyard on the Liddell family's farm specialises solely in sparkling wine.

Cottonworth's wines are produced with a blend of champagne and non-champagne grapes in the winery at nearby Hattingley Valley vineyard. A maze amongst the vines adds to the amusement for visitors to the vineyard.

WHITE

** (2) Classic Cuvée – NV
12.5% – (12.6 g/lt)
Oaked/Brut
Apple and almond aromas with a hint of brioche and minerality
Pinot Noir, Chardonnay, Pinot Meunier

ROSÉ

** (2) Brut Rosé – 2014
12.5% – (7.0 g/lt)
Oaked, summer fruit and quince aromas with vanilla and fresh acidity
Pinot Meunier (48%), Pinot Noir (47%), Pinot Noir Précoce (5%)

ROSEMARY

Smallbrook Lane, Ryde, PO33 4BE
01983 811084
rosemaryvineyard.co.uk

30 acres (approx. 1200 vines/acre)
First planted in 1986
Total wine production: approx. 80,000
bottles annually
Winemaker: Hans Schliefer

Terroir
Between 18m and 27m above sea level
Mostly south-facing slopes
Clay-silt loam soil over greensand

Visiting and buying
March to Dec, Tues to Sat, 10am to 4pm.
Guided tours 11am, 12noon, 1pm. Touring
park at vineyard. Wine sales at cellar door,
by mail order and online.

After Rossiter's vineyard was grubbed up a few years ago, Rosemary became the only commercial vineyard left on the Isle of Wight. Situated at Brading, a short walk from the railway station, it was the first vineyard planted on the island in the modern era and may actually reside on the site of a Roman vineyard, lying – as it does – close to the site of Roman remains. Rosemary is also one of the larger single-site vineyards in the UK. Its gentle, southerly facing slope is almost weatherproof; any early morning mists quickly roll off the site whilst the valley location acts as protection against south-westerly winds.

The award and medal-winning sparkling wines at Rosemary are made of champagne and non-champagne grapes, giving them a truly English style. On certain days during the year the vineyard is open for visitors to watch the 'work in progress'. White, rosé and red still wines, cider, liqueurs and fruit juices are also all produced at the vineyard.

WHITE

Brut – NV
12.0%
Pinot Gris, Seyval Blanc

ROSÉ

Sparkling Rosé – NV
12.0%
Brut
Crisp and light with rose petal aromas
Triomphe, Rondo, Phoenix

STANLAKE PARK

Twyford, RG10 0BN
01189 340176
stanlakepark.com

25 acres (approx. 1200 vines/acre)
First planted in 1979
Total wine production: approx. 35,000
bottles annually
Winemaker: Vince Gowe

Terroir
Between 37m and 73m above sea level
Mainly south-east facing slope
Loamy soils

Visiting and buying
Open all year, Fri, 4pm to 7pm, Sat and Sun
(and bank holidays), 12noon to 5pm; groups
by prior arrangement only; guided tours by
appointment, Sat and bank holidays, 2pm.
Wine sales at cellar door, online and at
selected local stockists.

Originally part of Windsor Great Park,
Stanlake Park vineyard was planted in the
late 1970s. It had several different vine/
grape varieties and utilised various different
systems of trellising and training. The
vineyard was different and experimental.
The first 500 vines were planted by
two early pioneers of modern English
winemaking, Jon Leighton and John
Worontschak. Gradually, over the years,
a number of small-scale developments
have taken the vineyard to its present

size. The grape-to-bottle winery, capable
of processing up to 500 tons of grapes, is
housed in a former barn dating from 1688.
The large capacity enables Stanlake Park to
make wine for other local vineyards.

Stanlake Park's own-label sparkling
wines are produced from a combination
of home-grown champagne and non-
champagne grapes. The guided tour and
tasting takes place on the hoof, with visitors
encouraged to drink and walk.

The vineyard also produces white, rosé and
red still wines.

WHITE

(1) Stanlake Brut – NV
12.0% – (2.5 g/lt)
Rich complex bouquet with creaminess on
the palate
Pinot Noir, Chardonnay, Gamay

(1) Heritage Brut – NV
12.5% – (4.8 g/lt)
Light bod./dry
Rich and creamy with crisp finish
Seyval Blanc, Müller-Thurgau,
Reichensteiner, Pinot Meunier

a'BECKETT'S

High Street, Littleton
Parnell, SN10 4EN
01380 816669
abecketts.co.uk

11 acres (approx. 1100 vines/acre)
First planted in 2001
Total wine production: approx. 15,000
bottles annually
Winemaker: Steve Brooksbank

Terroir
Between 50m and 75m above sea level
East to south-east facing slope
Greensand soil over chalk

Visiting and buying
Open all year, Weds to Sat (and bank
holidays), 11am to 4.30pm; groups by prior
arrangement only (summer months only);
guided tours by appointment. Wine sales
at cellar door, by mail order, online and at
selected local stockists.

a'Beckett's vineyard is situated in the Vale
of Pewsey, in a hidden valley to the north
of the chalk downs of Salisbury Plain. The
hillside opposite creates a rain shadow
that gives the vines here their own specific,
sheltered mesoclimate.

It was in 1999 that Paul Langham,
dissatisfied with corporate life, hit on the
idea of producing wine. Paul's wife Lynn
happened to find some land and in 2001
a new vineyard was created – initially with
5000 vines – and a change of lifestyle
accomplished. The vineyard was planted
with champagne and cool-climate non-
champagne grapes, and the first vintage
produced in 2003.

The vineyard also makes a white still wine,
cider and apple juice – produced from the
original orchards that comprise part of
what is an old fruit farm – as well as honey
from its bees.

WHITE

(1) Cuvée Victor – 2013
12.0% – (6.0 g/lt)
Brut
Fresh with white stone fruit and brioche
Seyval Blanc (80%), Chardonnay (11%),
Auxerrois (9%)

ROSÉ

(2) Cuvée Victoria – 2009
12.0% – (6.5 g/lt)
Brut
Soft fruit with brioche and soft finish
Seyval Blanc (65%), Pinot Noir (35%)

CHILTERN VALLEY

Dudley Lane, Hambleden, RG9 6JW
01491 638330
chilternvalley.co.uk

2.5 acres
First planted in 1982
Total wine production: 25,000 to 35,000 bottles annually
Winemaker: Neil Griffin

Terroir
Between 183m and 198m above sea level
Mainly east-facing steep slopes
Clay and chalk soils

Visiting and buying
Open all year; summer months, Mon to Fri, 9am to 6pm, Sat, Sun and bank holidays, 10am to 6pm; winter months, Mon to Fri, 9am to 5pm, Sat, Sun and bank holidays, 10am to 5pm; groups by prior arrangement only; guided tours by appointment, daily, 11am and 3pm. Cookery school. B&B at vineyard. Wine sales at cellar door, online, farmers' markets and selected local stockists.

Chiltern Valley Wines, part of the 'Old Luxters' site that includes a much-lauded brewery and cookery school, is set high in a well-wooded area overlooking the Hambleden Valley in the Chiltern Hills. The vineyard was planted by the present owner David Ealand in 1982. The winery, with its up-to-the-minute press and other equipment, is housed in the former stone and flint-built pigsty and grain store

of the original farm. The same building also houses the full-mash real ale brewery.

This small vineyard buys in grapes from surrounding vineyards, which, when added to the home-grown fruit, make up the annual production. The vineyard's own-label sparkling wines, made of champagne and non-champagne grapes, are vinified and stored offsite at Stanlake Park. These same own-label sparkling wines have received many trophies, awards and commendations in regional, national and international competitions, almost since the first vintage.

The vineyard also produces its own white, rosé and red still wines, and houses a liqueur distillery.

WHITE

Chiltern Valley Sparkling – 2013
12.0% – (4.5 g/lt)
Dry
Crisp and elegant with fresh fruit and balanced acidity
Chardonnay (50%), Pinot Noir (35%), Pinot Meunier (15%)

ROSÉ

Chiltern Valley Sparkling Rosé – 2013
13.0% – (5.5 g/lt)
Dry
Delicious and fruity with tinned strawberries and soft acidity
Cabernet Cortis (100%)

CHAFOR ESTATE

Preston Bissett Road,
Gawcott, MK18 4HT
01280 848583
chafor.co.uk

23 acres (approx. 1600 vines/acre)
First planted in 2009
Total wine production: approx. 10,000
bottles annually
Winemaker: Emma Rice

Terroir
Approx. 100m above sea level
Due-south aspect
Sand, gravel and flinty clay soil over
Jurassic limestone

Visiting and buying
Open all year, Fri and Sat, 11am to 4pm;
groups by prior arrangement only; self-
guided walkabout (when open); guided
tours, May to Sept, alternate Saturdays.
Wine sales at cellar door and at
selected national stockists.

High Hedges is one of the new wave of plantings made at the turn of the century that are now proving their worth. Sheltered by the Cotswolds to the west and the Chilterns to the south, the site benefits from low rainfall and relatively hot summers. This family-run vineyard has won a number of awards and medals at regional, national and international levels. In 2013 the owners bought a nearby vineyard and then, in 2017, extended their own acreage under vine. The winery was built in 2015.

In common with many recent English plantings, the champagne grapes have been selected to make the sparkling wines at the onsite winery. The vineyard also produces white and rosé still wines as well as a recently released brandy.

WHITE

(1) Vintage Cuvée – 2014
12.0% – (9.8 g/lt)
Brut
Spicy fruit and peach with baked apple and brioche
Pinot Noir (46%), Chardonnay (40%), Pinot Meunier (14%)

ROSÉ

(1) Vintage Rosé – 2014
12.0% – (7.4 g/lt)
Brut
Rose petal and strawberry/red cherry minerality
Pinot Meunier (52%), Pinot Noir (48%)

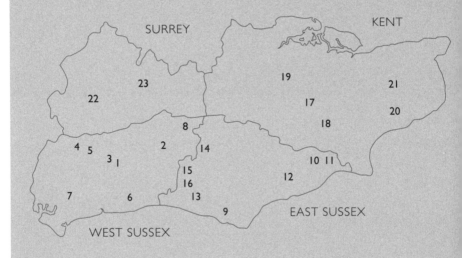

SURREY

KENT

19

22   23

21

17

20

8   18

4 5   2   14

3 1

10 11

15

16   12

7   6   13

9   EAST SUSSEX

WEST SUSSEX

3. SOUTH EAST

WEST SUSSEX
1. Nutbourne
2. Bolney Wine Estate
3. Nyetimber
4. Blackdown Ridge
5. Upperton
6. Wiston Estate
7. Tinwood Estate
8. Kingscote

EAST SUSSEX
9. Rathfinny Estate
10. Sedlescombe Organic
11. Oxney Organic Estate
12. Carr Taylor
13. Plumpton College
14. Bluebell Vineyard
15. Ridgeview Wine Estate
16. Court Garden

KENT
17. Biddenden
18. Chapel Down Wines
19. Hush Heath Estate
20. Terlingham
21. Elham Valley

SURREY
22. Albury Organic
23. Denbies Wine Estate

NUTBOURNE

Gay Street, West Chiltington, RH20 2HH
01798 815196
nutbournevineyards.com

26 acres (approx. 3000 vines/acre)
First planted in 1980
Total wine production: approx. 50,000
bottles annually
Winemaker: Owen Elais

Terroir
Approx. 107m above sea level
South-facing slopes
Greensand soils

Visiting and buying
May to Sept, Tues to Fri, 2pm to 5pm, Sat and
bank holidays, 11am to 5pm; Dec, Sat, 11am
to 4pm; groups by prior arrangement only;
self-guided walkabout (when open); guided
tours by appointment in summer months, Sat,
11am and 3pm. Wine sales at cellar door
and selected local stockists.

With a roaming herd of alpacas and
a distinctive windmill tasting room,
Nutbourne offers an unusual vineyard
experience. The vineyard has been owned
by the Gladwin family since 1991, and
expanded considerably in recent years, not
least with new plantings. Protected by the
South Downs, on the same road as the
Nyetimber Manor House and vineyard, the
area has its own distinct microclimate.

The sparkling wines are made from
champagne grapes in the vineyard's winery.
Nutbourne has established a considerable
reputation, with its wine being served
at Buckingham Palace and Westminster.
Visitors are free to roam around the lakes
and vines at their leisure. The vineyard also
produces white, rosé and red still wines.

WHITE

* Nutty – 2014
12.0% – (5.0 g/lt)
Brut
Excellent white stone fruit, zesty and balanced
Pinot Noir (70%), Chardonnay (30%)

** (1) Nutty Wild – NV
10.0% – (0.0 g/lt)
Brut
Nature – soft red berry with citrus back edge
Pinot Noir

ROSÉ

Nutty Blush – 2010
12.0% – (6.0 g/lt)
Brut
Full fruity
Pinot Noir (70%), Chardonnay (30%)

BOLNEY WINE ESTATE

Bookers Vineyard, Foxhole Lane,
Bolney, RH17 5NB
01444 881575
bolneywineestate.com

**39 acres (between 1000 and 1400
vines/acre)**
First planted in 1972
**Total wine production: approx. 300,000
bottles annually**
**Winemakers: Samantha Linter,
Alex Rabagliata and Liz Garrett**

Terroir
Between 18m and 55m above sea level
South-facing slope
Medium loam over ancient slate

Visiting and buying
*Open all year, Tues to Sat, 9am to 5pm;
groups by prior arrangement only; guided
tours by appointment.* Wine sales at cellar
door, online and at selected national
stockists.

The Bolney Wine Estate story began
in 1972, when Janet and Rodney Pratt
planted three acres of vines on a former
pig farm on the edge of the South
Downs. Today, this self-sufficient business
comprises five vineyard sites, totalling
almost forty acres in size, run by Janet and
Rodney's daughter, Samantha. A recently
built tasting room and shop, along with
vineyard trail, add to the welcoming feel of
a very well-organised vineyard.

Bolney grows many grape varieties – both
champagne and non-champagne – for their
white, rosé and, unusually, red sparkling
wines. Recently, the vineyard created a
white and a rosé as own-label sparkling
wines for Kew Gardens. Over the years,
the vineyard has won many regional,
national and international awards and
medals for its sparkling wines. The vineyard
also produces several white, rosé and red
still wines, a vermouth and a gin.

WHITE

*(1) Bubbly – NV
12.5% – (9.0 g/lt)
Brut
Light and refreshing with elderflower creaminess
Müller-Thurgau, Chardonnay, Seyval Blanc

**(1) Blanc de Blancs – 2015
12.5% – (9.0 g/lt)
Full bod./Brut
Citrus fruit character with yeasty undertones
Chardonnay (100%)

Classic Cuvée – 2013
10.5% – (12.0 g/lt)
Brut
Floral and brioche notes with zesty apple and citrus
Chardonnay (55%), Pinot Noir (43%), Pinot Meunier (2%)

Blanc de Noirs – 2015
13.0% – (6.0 g/lt)
Brut
Stone fruit with honey and pear notes
Pinot Noir (95%), Pinot Meunier (5%)

Kew English Sparkling – NV
12.5% – (8.0 g/lt)
Brut
Floral and zesty citrus with honeysuckle and elderflower
Reichensteiner, Müller-Thurgau, Chardonnay

ROSÉ

** (1) Cuvée Rosé – 2014
12.5% – (9.0 g/lt)
Full bod./Brut
Blackberry fruit with yeasty undertones
Pinot Noir (100%)

Eighteen Acre – NV
13.0% – (11.5 g/lt)
Brut
Ripe strawberries and red cherries with sweet spice
Rondo

Kew English Sparkling – NV
12.5% – (12.0 g/lt)
Brut
Raspberry and wild strawberry with savoury undertone
Pinot Noir, Gamay

RED

* (1) Cuvée Noir – 2013
12.5% – (9.0 g/lt)
Full bod./Brut
Aromas of red stone fruits with summer fruits
Dornfelder (100%)

West Sussex

NYETIMBER

Gay Street, West Chiltington, RH20 2HH
01798 813989
nyetimber.com

650 acres across several sites
(between 1600 and 2700 vines/acre)
First planted in 1988
Total wine production: approx. 1.3 million
bottles annually
Winemakers: Cherie Spriggs
and Brad Greatrix

Terroir
Approx. 60m above sea level
South-facing slopes
Greensand over chalk soil

Visiting and buying
The vineyard has three weekend
openings (by ticket), one each in June,
Aug and Sept. Wine sales at selected
national stockists

When two Americans, Stuart and Sandra Moss, planted Chardonnay, Pinot Noir and Pinot Meunier vines on a thirty-nine-acre plot adjacent to their house in 1988, the wine press thought they were mad. However, when their first vintage, the 1992 Premier Cuvée, won gold in the 1997 International Wine and Spirit Competition, a new era in English winemaking was born.

Nyetimber Manor, in the lee of the South Downs, is mentioned in the Domesday book, and the current incarnation of the house has a chequered history, having been under the ownership, variously, of Anne of Cleves and, for a short time, Andy Hill, of Bucks Fizz fame. The property and attendant vineyard were bought by the present owner, Eric Hereema, in 2006. Eric has maintained the Moss' emphasis on quality, and has increased the planting at Nyetimber and other sites – retaining the exclusivity of those three grape varieties – to its current, expansive size. The wines at Nyetimber are vinified and stored at the vineyard's newly built onsite winery.

WHITE

Classic Cuvée – MV
12.0% – (9.0 g/lt)
Brut
Toasty and spicy aromas with honey, almond and baked apple flavours
Chardonnay, Pinot Noir, Pinot Meunier

Blanc de Blancs – 2010
12.0% – (10.0 g/lt)
Mid to full bod./Brut
Light citrus and stonefruit with zippy apple and citrus
Chardonnay (100%)

Tillington Single Vineyard – 2013
12.0% – (9.7 g/lt)
Brut
Redcurrant and wild raspberry with almond, brioche and minerality
Chardonnay (100%)

Demi-Sec – MV
12.0% – (44.0 g/lt)
Mineral, lemon, honey and tangerine with crisp acidity
Chardonnay

ROSÉ

Rosé – MV
12.0% – (11.0 g/lt)
Brut
Red mango, honey and liquorice with cherry and redcurrants
Pinot Noir, Chardonnay, Pinot Meunier

BLACKDOWN RIDGE

Blackdown Park, Hazelmere,
GU27 3BT
01428 656003
blackdownridge.co.uk

10.5 acres (approx. 2700 vines/acre)
First planted in 2010
Total wine production: approx. 14,000
bottles annually
Winemaker: Josh Hammond

Terroir
Approx. 135m above sea level
Steep south-easterly facing slopes
Chalky soils

Visiting and buying
Open by appointment only; guided tours
by appointment. Wine sales at cellar door,
online and at selected local stockists

Set on the highest stretch of the Sussex
Weald, overlooking the South Downs
National Park, the vineyard at Blackdown
Ridge is the result of a discussion between
Professor Martin Cook, the owner, and
Antonio, a friend from an Italian winemaking family. The sparkling wines are
produced at the vineyard's winery from
the three classic champagne grapes. The
vineyard also produces white, rosé and red
still wines.

WHITE

Primordia – 2014
11.0% – (7.0 g/lt)
Lemon sherbet and apricot notes with
orchard fruit and sweet pastry
Pinot Noir (51%), Chardonnay (39%),
Pinot Meunier (10%)

ROSÉ

Sparkling Rosé – 2015
11.0% – (3.0 g/lt)
Brut
Strawberry and floral notes with red berry
and white peach
Pinot Noir (95%), Pinot Meunier (5%)

UPPERTON

Tillington, GU28 0RD
01798 343695
uppertonvineyards.co.uk

4 acres (approx. 1250 vines/acre)
First planted in 2005
Total wine production: between 5000 and
10,000 bottles annually
Winemaker: Simon Roberts

Terroir
Between 40m and 90m above sea level
South-facing slope
Lower greensand soils

Visiting and buying
April to Christmas, Tues to Thurs, 12noon to
5pm, Fri and Sat, 10am to 5pm; other times
by appointment; groups by prior arrangement
only; guided tours by appointment, May to
Sept, Sat, 2pm. Wine sales at cellar door and
selected stockists.

When Andy Rodgers planted his first 800
vines of Rondo, Pinot Noir Précoce and
Chardonnay, he intended to produce still
wine, but it wasn't long before he decided
to specialise in sparkling. The vineyard
is now a family concern, run with his
daughter and grandson on the south-facing
slopes overlooking the South Downs.

All the sparkling wines at Upperton are
blends of champagne and non-champagne
grapes, and are vinified at Ridgeview Wine
Estate (see page 82).

WHITE

Alia – 2013
12.0% – (8.0 g/lt)
Brut
Brioche, apple, yellow plum with complex, rich
flavours
Chardonnay (100%)

Aurora – 2014
12.0% – (8.0 g/lt)
Full bod./Brut
Brioche, toasty aromas with balanced fruit
and acidity
Chardonnay (51%), Pinot Noir (29%),
Pinot Meunier (20%)

** Nebula – 2014
12.5% – (8.8 g/lt)
Brut
Peach, apple, strawberry, brioche with
refreshing finish
Pinot Noir (58%), Chardonnay (26%),
Pinot Meunier (16%)

Tenebris – 2014
12.0% – (10.0 g/lt)
Brut
Confected cherry and pear drops with anise
and liquorice
Pinot Noir (85%), Pinot Meunier (15%)

ROSÉ

**Erubesco – 2013
12.5% – (10.0g/lt)
Brut
Ripe berries, green apples, citrus with zesty finish
Pinot Noir (47%), Pinot Meunier (32%),
Pinot Noir Précoce (20%), Chardonnay (1%)

WISTON ESTATE

North Farm, London Road, Washington,
RH20 4BB
01903 812129
wistonestate.com

16 acres (approx. 1600 vines/acre)
First planted in 2006
Total wine production: around 30,000
bottles annually
Winemaker: Dermot Sugrue

Terroir
Approx. 100m above sea level
South-facing slope
Upper Cretaceous chalk soils

Visiting and buying
April to Oct, by appointment; groups by
prior arrangement only; guided tours by
appointment, April to Oct. Wine sales at
cellar door, online and at selected national
stockists.

Pip Goring, along with husband Harry,
has fulfilled a lifelong ambition to create a
vineyard at the family home, to remind her
of her South African roots. The vineyard
comprises sixteen acres of the wider 6000-
acre farm that has been in the Goring
family since the 1700s.

Wiston is situated on a gentle south-facing
slope that forms the side of a dried-up
river bed. Having planted the site with the
three principal champagne grape varieties
in 2006, the owners' sole aim for Wiston
is to produce top-quality sparkling wines.
The acquisition of several regional, national
and international awards and medals in the
vineyard's short history, confirms that their
ambition has been realised.

Dermot Sugrue, domiciled and visiting
consultant winemaker, has established
a unique winery at Wiston. He is the
only UK-based winemaker to use a
traditional-design Coquard basket-grape
press, from which the resulting juices pass
slowly, fed by gravity, to the initial three-
section stainless steel fermentation tanks
situated on the floor below. The gentle
pressing process, with no 'intervention
of movement', is thought to produce the
purest juice. Vinification then follows on
conventional lines.

WHITE

(2) Cuvée – 2013
12.0% – (8.0 g/lt)
Brut
Yeasty aromas, hints of roasted nuts and apple with fresh acidity
Pinot Noir (47%), Chardonnay (33%), Pinot Meunier (20%)

(1) Brut – NV
12.0% – (6.0 g/lt)
Toasty and savoury, yeasty and bready
Chardonnay, Pinot Noir, Pinot Meunier

(1) Blanc de Blancs – 2010
12.0% – (8.0 g/lt)
Dry
Passion fruit and pineapple with baked apple and buttered teacakes
Chardonnay (100%)

(1) Blanc de Blancs – NV
12.0% – (9.0 g/lt)
Brut
Green apple with racy citrus finish
Chardonnay

(2) Blanc de Noirs – 2010
12.0% – (9.0 g/lt)
Full bod./Dry
Fruit driven
Pinot Noir (100%)

Estate Blanc de Noirs – NV
12.0% – (8.0 g/lt)
Brut
Fruit-driven flavours
Pinot Noir

ROSÉ

(2) Rosé – 2014
12.0% – (10.0g/lt)
Brut
Tart red fruit and dairy notes with crisp profile
Pinot Noir (68%), Pinot Meunier (22%), Chardonnay (10%)

(2) Rosé – NV
12.0% – (11.0g/lt)
Dry
Red berries, creamy textured
Chardonnay, Pinot Noir

TINWOOD ESTATE

Tinwood Lane, Halnaker, PO18 0NE
01243 537372
tinwoodestate.com

65 acres (approx. 1700 vines/acre)
First planted in 2007
Total wine production: approx. 30,000
bottles annually
Winemakers: Simon Roberts
and Art Tukker

Terroir
Approx. 35m above sea level
South-westerly orientation
Stony soil over chalk

Visiting and buying
Open year round, daily, 10am to 6pm; groups
by prior arrangement only; guided tours, Mon
to Fri, 3pm, Sat and Sun, 12noon. B&B lodges
at vineyard. Wine sales at cellar door, online
(case only) and at selected local speciality
outlets.

Tinwood has its own microclimate, sitting
snugly, as it does, in the rain shadow of the
South Downs, only three miles from the
sea. The site was planted adjacent to the
Goodwood Estate in 2007, on what was
an iceberg lettuce farm. Tinwood places
emphasis on ensuring its wine production
is as environmentally sound as possible;
for example, planting bee-friendly flowers
along the rows of vines.

Only the three principal champagne grape
varieties have been planted at Tinwood. The
wines are vinified at, and by, Ridgeview Wine
Estate (see page 82), and then matured
onsite at Tinwood.

The vineyard also produces its own honey.

WHITE

** (1) Estate Brut – 2015
12.0% – (7.5 g/lt)
Citrus and melon with hints of honey and brioche
Chardonnay (50%), Pinot Noir (30%), Pinot
Meunier (20%)

** (1) Blanc de Blancs – 2015
12.0% – (7.5 g/lt)
Brut
Green apple flavours, tropical fruit and soft
minerality
Chardonnay (100%)

ROSÉ

** (1) Rosé – 2015
12.0% – (9.2 g/lt)
Brut
Red forest fruits with raspberries and
strawberries and cream
Pinot Noir (60%), Pinot Meunier (20%),
Chardonnay (20%)

KINGSCOTE

Mill Place Farm, Vowels Lane,
East Grinstead, RH19 4LG
01342 327535
kingscoteestate.com

15 acres (approx. 1700 vines/acre)
First planted in 2010
Total wine production: up to 100,000
bottles annually
Winemaker: Owen Elias

Terroir
Between 70m and 80m above sea level
South-facing slopes
Sandy, clay and ironstone soils

Visiting and buying
Open all year, daily, 9.30am to 5.30pm;
groups by prior arrangement only; guided
tours by appointment, April to Sept, daily.
Cookery school, livery stables, clay shooting,
fishing. Holiday cottages at vineyard. Wine
sales at cellar door and online.

The fifteen-acre vineyard at Kingscote,
planted in 2010 by a previous owner, forms
part of a 150-acre Wealden Valley estate
that traces its origins back to 1380. The
whistle of a steam engine drifts over now
and again, from the Kingscote Station on
the nearby Bluebell Railway. Set amongst
rolling hills, a winding river and numerous
fishing lakes, the vines here support
authorised champagne grapes. The current
owner has plans to enlarge the vineyard, to
better utilise the Kingscote winery.

The vineyard also produces white still
wines and a sparkling cyder.

WHITE

Cuvée Christen – NV
12.0% – (5.0 g/lt)
Brut
Citrus and lime with apple, lemon and white
chocolate
Pinot Noir, Pinot Meunier, Chardonnay,
Pinot Blanc

East Sussex

RATHFINNY ESTATE

Alfriston, BN26 5TU
01323 871031
rathfinnyestate.com

72 acres (approx. 1600 vines/acre)
First planted in 2010
Total wine production: approx. 100,000
bottles annually
Winemaker: Jonathan Medard

Terroir
Between 30m and 80m above sea level
South-facing slope
Chalky soils

Visiting and buying
Open all year, daily, 10am to 4pm; groups by
prior arrangement only; guided tours, April and
May, Fri, Sat and Sun. Wine sales at cellar
door and at selected stockists.

Situated in the Cradle Valley, overlooking the
South Downs National Park, Rathfinny boasts
a spectacular location for its vines. Owner
Mark Driver had already started a course
in Wine Production at Plumpton College
when Rathfinny Farm came up for sale. Today,
after an eight-year development period, the
vines on the farm are bearing fruit and the
fully self-sufficient vineyard is producing its
first sparkling wines. The energy-efficient site
continues to progress steadily, with further
facilities and vines being added gradually. At
present, seventy-two acres of the 600-acre
estate have been planted, with the remainder
of the land open for exploration.

Rathfinny's sparkling wine is made of
champagne grapes in the onsite winery. The
vineyard also produces a white still wine, a
gin and a vermouth.

WHITE

** Blanc de Blancs – 2014
12.5% – (4.0 g/lt)
Brut
Apricot and acacia notes with lemon and
apple strudel
Chardonnay (100%)

** Blanc de Noirs – 2015
12% – (4.5 g/lt)
Brut
Peony and wild strawberry with raspberry,
almonds and red apple
Pinot Noir (65%), Pinot Meunier (35%)

ROSÉ

** Rosé – 2015
12.5% – (2.5 g/lt)
Brut
Strawberries and cream minerality with
peachy finish
Pinot Noir (50%), Chardonnay (40%),
Pinot Meunier (10%)

SEDLESCOMBE ORGANIC

Hawkhurst Road, Cripp's Corner,
Sedlescombe, TN32 5SA
01580 830715
englishbiodynamicwine.co.uk

22 acres
First planted in 1979
Total wine production: approx. 30,000
bottles annually
Winemaker: Roy Cook

Terroir
Between 60m and 120m above sea level
South-facing slopes
Sandy loam soils

Visiting and buying
Open all year, daily, 10.30am to 5.30pm;
groups by prior arrangement only, March
to Oct; self-guided walkabout (when open),
March to Oct. Woodland nature trail. Wine
sales at cellar door.

In 1979, Roy Cook, then a casual organic
gardener, planted 1.5 acres of vines a few
miles north of Hastings, in what is now the
High Weald AONB. The farm was inherited
from Roy's grandfather and sits amongst
wartime defence installations. Sedlescombe
was certified organic from the beginning,
becoming the first such vineyard in the
UK. Today, expanded to twenty-two acres,
and under the new ownership of Sophie
and Kieran Balmer, the vineyard uses
champagne and non-champagne home-
grown grapes to produce sparkling wines
in its own winery.

Sedlescombe is farmed biodynamically – an
approach that shuns the use of chemicals
in the same way that organic farming does,
but which also incorporates lunar and
cosmic rhythms to the benefit of soil and
plants. The vineyard is also a member of
WWOOF, an organisation that encourages
volunteers to learn about – and work
in – organic agriculture, including wine
production.

The vineyard also produces white, rosé and
red still wines together with a dessert wine.

WHITE

Pinot Noir/Chardonnay – 2013
11.2% – (8.8 g/lt)
Brut
Fresh tangy tropical fruit with yeast and oaty
notes
Pinot Noir (66%), Chardonnay (34%)

ROSÉ

(1) Rosé Brut – 2013
11.3% – (6.5g/lt)
Tangy tropical fruit and yeast with red fruit
flavours and toasty notes
Rondo (78%), Pinot Noir (22%)

East Sussex

OXNEY ORGANIC ESTATE

Little Bellhurst Farm, Hobbs Lane, Beckley,
TN31 6TU
01797 260137
oxneyestate.com

34.5 acres (approx. 1500 vines/acre)
First planted in 2012
Total wine production: approx. 23,000
bottles annually
Winemaker: Ben Smith

Terroir
Approx. 17m above sea level
South-west facing slope
Tunbridge Wells Sand and silt-loam soil

Visiting and buying
March to Nov, Tues to Fri, 10am to 4pm;
groups by prior arrangement only; guided
tours, March to Nov, first and third Fri each
month, 10am and 12noon. Self-catering
cottages and shepherd's huts at vineyard.
Wine sales at cellar door, online and at
selected local stockists.

Sloping down to the River Rother, and
overlooking the river's floodplain, this
twenty-one-acre vineyard forms part of a
much larger organic arable farm. The vines
at Oxney were planted in 2012 and the
sparkling wines, made solely from home-
grown champagne grapes, have already
won awards. The modern winery is located
in a converted square oast house, and the
other facilities, all attractive features of the
vineyard, are similarly housed in restored
buildings.

The vineyard also produces a rosé still wine.

WHITE

(1) Classic – 2015
11.5% – (5.0 g/lt)
Oaked/Dry
Elegant and fruit-driven with toast and
brioche notes
Pinot Noir (51%), Pinot Meunier (29%),
Chardonnay (20%)

ROSÉ

(1) Estate Rosé – 2016
11.5% – (10.0 g/lt)
Dry
Fresh and lively with crisp finish
Pinot Noir (100%)

CARR TAYLOR

Wheel Lane, Westfield, TN35 4SG
01424 752501
carr-taylor.co.uk

37 acres (between 450 and 1000 vines/acre)
First planted in 1971
Total wine production: between 40,000
and 50,000 bottles annually
Winemakers: Alex Carr Taylor
and Liam Tilston

Terroir
Approx. 40m above sea level
South-east facing slopes
Ore/clay shale soil over sandstone

Visiting and buying
Open all year, daily, 10am to 5pm; groups by
prior arrangement only; self-guided tours when
open; guided tours by appointment. Wine
sales at cellar door, by phone and mail order,
online and at selected local stockists.

David Carr Taylor planted his vineyard,
initially twenty-one acres, in 1971–72
as a cash crop for his existing farm. The
first crop was harvested in the legendary,
blazing summer of 1976. Further planting
in recent years has expanded the vineyard
to its present size. Although lying just a
few miles from the coast, the vineyard is
sheltered by rolling countryside and well-
positioned windbreaks.

Having produced the first commercially
available sparkling rosé wine in the UK,
the vineyard is now in the hands of the
family's second-generation winemaker. The
sparkling wines produced at the vineyard
winery are a blending of champagne and
non-champagne grapes.

The vineyard also produces white and rosé
still wines, as well as mead.

WHITE

(1) Brut – NV
12.0% – (9.0 g/lt)
Full bod.
Apple, elderflower and biscuit with crisp green
apple and butter
Reichensteiner, Schönburger

(1) Pinot Blanc – 2013
12.0% – (4.0 g/lt)
Brut
White peach and brioche with mineral white
fruit and apricot
Pinot Noir (50%), Pinot Blanc (50%)

(3) Demi-Sec – 2014
12.0% – (33.0 g/lt)
Soft peach with apple, vanilla and fresh fruit
Reichensteiner (60%), Schönburger (40%)

ROSÉ

(2) Rosé – NV
12.0% – (7.0 g/lt)
Dry
Redcurrants and raspberries with red berries
and cherry
Pinot Noir, Pinot Meunier

PLUMPTON COLLEGE

Ditchling Road, Lewes, BN7 3AE
01273 892094
plumpton.ac.uk

15 acres (approx. 1400 vines/acre)
First planted in 1988
Total wine production: 18,000 bottles
annually
Winemaker: Sarah Midgley

Terroir
Approx. 30m above sea level
South-facing slopes
Poorly drained clay soil over clay subsoil

Visiting and buying
Visits by appointment only; groups by prior
arrangement. Wine sales at selected local
stocklists and online.

Plumpton College was founded in 1926 as
an agricultural teaching facility. In 1988, it
planted its first vineyard within the college
grounds, thus opening its wine educational
facility. The vines benefit from Plumpton's
location, sheltering in the rain shadow of
the South Downs.

Initially, students at the college were given
two rows of vines to produce their own
wine, which they could dispose of at their
will. Today's students produce consistent
collegiate wines under supervision; the
wines are then sold to supplement college
funds, enabling the further development of
wine industry courses. Many of the UK's
current crop of winemakers have attended
the college at some point in their careers.
Various Plumpton College sparkling wines
have received awards and medals at the
Champagne & Sparkling Wine World
Championships and from Wines of Great
Britain, as well as other industry judging
panels. Plumpton also produces white and
rosé still wines.

WHITE

Estate Brut Classic – NV
12.0% – (8.0 g/lt)
Crisp apple and citrus with creamy brioche
Pinot Meunier, Chardonnay, Pinot Noir

ROSÉ

Estate Brut Rosé – NV
12.0% – (10.0 g/lt)
White peach and strawberry with creamy
brioche
Pinot Noir

BLUEBELL VINEYARD

Glenmore Farm, Sliders Lane, Furners
Green, TN22 3RU
01825 791561
bluebellvineyard.co.uk

84 acres (approx. 1200 vines/acre)
First planted in 2005
Total wine production: around 50,000
bottles annually
Winemaker: Kevin Sutherland

Terroir
Between 55m and 75m above sea level
East, south and west-facing slopes
Sandy loam soil over sandstone

Visiting and buying
Open all year, Mon to Sat, 10am to
4pm; groups by prior arrangement
only; self-guided walkabout when open;
guided tours, March to Oct, selected
Thurs, Fri or Sat. Wine sales at cellar
door, online and at selected national
stockists.

Photo: Justin Hewes

This vineyard takes its name from the Bluebell woods, not the adjacent steam railway. A family-owned former pig farm on the edge of Ashdown Forest, the vineyard has grown steadily in size since the first planting in 2005. It's one of a number that form a comprehensively managed vineyard estate.

Bluebell Vineyard solely produces sparkling wine, made both from champagne and non-champagne grapes. Being vintage in style, the palate of the wine may vary from year to year. Individually, the wines have received many regional, national and international awards and medals over the short life of the vineyard.

WHITE

Classic Cuvée – 2014
11.5% – (2.1 g/lt)
Brut
Elderflower and spice with mandarin, pink grapefruit and pear
Chardonnay (61%), Pinot Noir (24%), Pinot Meunier (15%)

** (2) Blanc de Blancs – 2014
11.5% – (9.1 g/lt)
Brut
Aromas of ripe apple and lemon with lemon curd and pink grapefruit
Chardonnay (100%)

* (1) Seyval Blanc – 2013
11.5% – (5.9 g/lt)
Brut
Elderflower and orange blossom with apple, grapefruit and pear
Seyval Blanc (100%)

* Barrel Aged Blanc de Blancs – 2013
11.5% – (7.1 g/lt)
Oaked/Brut
Spicy notes of vanilla and citrus with plum, pineapple and almond
Chardonnay (100%)

* Late Disgorged Blanc de Blancs – 2008
11.5% – (5.0 g/lt)
Brut
Lemon and lime citrus with red fruits and brioche
Chardonnay (100%)

ROSÉ

* (2) Rosé – 2013
11.5% – (5.4 g/lt)
Brut
Red cherries and wild strawberries
Pinot Noir (77%), Pinot Meunier (23%)

RIDGEVIEW WINE ESTATE

Fragbarrow Lane, Ditchling Common,
BN6 8TP
01444 242040
ridgeview.co.uk

30 acres (approx. 900 vines/acre)
First planted in 1995
Total wine production: approx. 250,000
bottles annually
Winemaker: Simon Roberts

Terroir
Between 40m and 50m above sea level
Generally south-facing slope
Clay soil over limestone and sandstone

Visiting and buying
Open all year, Mon to Sun, 11am to
4pm; groups by prior arrangement only;
guided tours by appointment. Wine
sales at cellar door, online and at
selected stockists.

The conditions in Ditchling, home to the Ridgeview Wine Estate, with its cool climate and unique geology, sitting snugly at the foot of the South Downs, lend themselves perfectly to the production of sparkling wine.

Ridgeview was one of the first English vineyards to focus solely on sparkling wine. Mike Roberts and his wife, Christine, planted an initial sixteen acres of vines in 1995, and chose to cultivate only the traditional champagne grapes. Sadly, Mike passed away in 2015, four years after being made an MBE for his services to the English wine industry. Today, the second generation of the Roberts family maintains the Ridgeview reputation for top-quality sparkling wines. The vineyard has won numerous trophies, not least the Viticulture Grower of the Year award in 2017 and the IWSC 2018 Winemaker of the Year award. Their wines have been served at both No.10 Downing Street and Buckingham Palace.

WHITE

(1) Cavendish – NV
12.0% – (8.0 g/lt)
Brut
Hints of red fruits then fruit focussed with biscuit and bread
Pinot Noir, Pinot Meunier, Chardonnay

(2) Bloomsbury – NV
12.0% – (8.8 g/lt)
Brut
Citrus fruit aromas with melon and honey then crisp fruit
Chardonnay, Pinot Noir, Pinot Meunier

Blanc de Noirs – 2014
12.0% – (9.0 g/lt)
Brut
Red fruit aromas with sweet spice and fresh herbs
Pinot Noir (68%), Pinot Meunier (32%)

** Blanc de Blancs – 2014
12.0% – (9.0 g/lt)
Brut
Honey and brioche with citrus, white tropical fruit and minerality
Chardonnay (100%)

ROSÉ

(2) Fitzrovia – NV
12.0% – (10.0 g/lt)
Brut
Raspberry and redcurrant nose with strawberries and cream
Chardonnay, Pinot Noir, Pinot Meunier

Rosé de Noirs – 2014
12.0% – (10.0 g/lt)
Brut
Summer fruits, alongside honey and toast
Pinot Noir (74%), Pinot Meunier (26%)

East Sussex

COURT GARDEN

Orchard Lane, Ditchling, BN6 8TH
01273 844479
courtgarden.com

17 acres (approx. 1600 vines/acre)
First planted in 2005
Total wine production: approx. 25,000
bottles annually
Winemaker: Hugh Corney

Terroir
Between 60m and 80m above sea level
South-facing slope
Clay and greensand soils

Visiting and buying
*Open all year, Tues, Weds and Sat, 9am to
2pm, Thurs and Fri, 9am to 5pm; groups
by prior arrangement only; guided tours
by appointment, Sat, 11am; tastings by
appointment, Sat, 3pm. Wine sales at
cellar door, by mail order, online and at
selected local stockists.*

All six of the permitted champagne grapes have been planted in the Court Garden vineyard – with Pinot Gris, Pinot Blanc and Petit Meslier included alongside the 'usual' three. Planted as a single-estate vineyard and winery on the family farm in 2005, in the lee of the South Downs, the enterprise is now in the hands of the second-generation winemaker.

Court Garden has built a considerable reputation at home and abroad, winning several regional, national and international medals and awards. Alongside the sparkling wine, made from a combination of the six aforementioned grape varieties, the vineyard also produces white, rosé and red still wines.

WHITE

** (1) Classic Cuvée – 2014
12.0% – (4.5 g/lt)
Brut
Toasty under ripe pineapple, greengage and creamy finish
Pinot Noir (43%), Chardonnay (36%), Pinot Meunier (21%)

(1) Ditchling Reserve – 2014
12.0% – (9.0 g/lt)
Oaked/Brut
Rich and honeyed with spicy red fruit and juicy acidity
Pinot Noir (90%), Pinot Meunier (10%)

(1) Blanc de Blancs – 2014
12.0% – (9.0 g/lt)
Extra dry
Ripe peach and apple fruits with off-dry crisp finish
Chardonnay (100%)

(1) Blanc de Noirs – 2013
11.0% – (9.0 g/lt)
Brut
Green fruit and lemongrass accent with good balance
Pinot Noir (73%), Pinot Meunier (27%)

ROSÉ

** Rosé – 2013
11.0% – (9.0 g/lt)
Brut
Dried cranberry with defined red fruit and lively acidity
Pinot Noir (65%), Pinot Meunier (35%)

BIDDENDEN

Gribble Bridge Lane, Biddenden,
TN27 8DF
01580 291726
biddendenvineyards.com

**23 acres (between 1000 and 1200 vines/
acre)**
First planted in 1969
**Total wine production: approx. 80,000
bottles annually**
Winemaker: Julian Barnes

Terroir
Between 52m and 65m above sea level
South-facing slope
Sandy loam soils over Wealden Clay

Visiting and buying
*Open all year, Mon to Sat, 10am to
5pm, Sun and bank holidays, 11am to
5pm (closed on Sundays in Jan and Feb);
groups by prior arrangement only; self-
guided walkabout (when open); guided
tours by appointment. Wine sales at
cellar door and online.*

Biddenden, originally planted on a third of an acre of land by the Barnes family in 1969, was the first such vineyard in Kent. Today, the site has grown to twenty-four acres within the wider seventy-acre estate. Facing south on the side of a small, sheltered, gently sloping valley where visitors are at liberty to roam, the microclimate at Biddenden is well suited for growing grapes. The vineyard remains operated and managed by the Barnes family, today in its third generation. The grape varieties grown and the system of trellising used may have changed with experience of the climate and soils, but the quality of the wine has remained throughout.

The sparkling wines produced at the Biddenden winery are all made of champagne and non-champagne grapes, and have won many medals and awards at regional, national and international competitions. The vineyard also produces white, rosé and red still wines, cider and honey.

WHITE

(2) Gribble Bridge White – 2013
12.0% – (12.0 g/lt)
Dry
Soft fruit with creamy white fleshy fruit finish
Reichensteiner (60%), Pinot Noir (30%), Scheurebe (10%)

(1) Pinot Reserve – 2014
11.0% – (8.0 g/lt)
Brut
Rich and creamy with hints of brioche
Pinot Noir (100%)

ROSÉ

(3) Gribble Bridge Rosé – 2014
11.0%
Off dry
Strawberry, raspberry and pear with half squeeze of lemon
Gamay (100%)

CHAPEL DOWN WINES

Small Hythe, Tenterden, TN30 7NG
01580 763033
chapeldown.com

**370 acres (between 1200 and
1700 vines/acre)**
First planted in 1977
**Total wine production: approx. 700,000
bottles annually**
Winemaker: Josh Donaghay-Spire

Terroir
Between 9m and 18m above sea level
Mainly south facing
Wealden Clay and chalky soils

Visiting and buying
*Open all year, daily, 10am to 5pm; groups by
prior arrangement only; guided tours, April to
Nov, daily, 10.30am and 3.15pm.* Wine sales
at cellar door, by mail order, online and at
selected national stockists.

Originally developed as a winery by
Stephen Skelton, for the processing of
grapes brought in from any number of
surrounding vineyards, Tenterden (as it was
known) then planted its own vineyard to
supplement the supply of grapes. Over the
years, the vineyard planting has continued,
further expanding the site. Chapel
Down, as Tenterden became, has its own
familiar label of award-winning sparkling
wines, made both from champagne and
non-champagne grapes. The winery also
continues to vinify grapes on behalf of
other vineyards.

Chapel Down also produces white, rosé
and red still wines, and has a gin distillery
and a brewery.

WHITE

* (1) Classic – NV
12.0% – (7.5 g/lt)
Brut
Lemongrass, red apple and baked bread with strawberry and quince
Pinot Noir, Chardonnay, Pinot Blanc, Pinot Meunier

** (2) Century Extra Dry – NV
12.0% – (16.0 g/lt)
Extra Sec
Baked apple, sherbet, elderflower nose
Pinot Noir, Chardonnay, Pinot Blanc, Pinot Meunier

** (1) Three Graces – 2013
12.0% – (10.0 g/lt)
Brut
Ripe apple aromas and strawberry with brioche and hazelnut
Chardonnay (60%), Pinot Noir (29%), Pinot Meunier (11%)

Kit's Coty Blanc de Blancs – 2013
12.0% – (9.0 g/lt)
Oaked/Brut
Green apple and baked bread with toasty character
Chardonnay (100%)

(1) Kit's Coty Coeur de Cuvée – 2013
12.0% – (6.0 g/lt)
Oaked
Spiced apple with tropical fruit, chalky minerality and tangy acidity
Chardonnay (100%)

ROSÉ

Rosé – NV
12.0% – (8.0 g/lt)
Brut
Lemon sherbet nose with blackcurrant, rosehip and strawberry
Pinot Noir

HUSH HEATH ESTATE

Five Oak Lane, Staplehurst, TN12 0HT
01622 832794
hushheath.com

130 acres (approx. 1400 vines/acre)
First planted in 2002
Total wine production: approx. 150,000
bottles annually
Winemakers: Victoria Ash and Owen Elias

Terroir
Approx. 150m above sea level
Mostly south-facing slopes
Wealden Clay over Tunbridge Wells
Sandstone

Visiting and buying
Open all year, daily, 11am to 4pm; groups by
prior arrangement only; self-guided walkabout
(when open); guided tours, April to Oct, Sun
to Thurs, 11am and 2.30pm. Wine sales at
cellar door, online and selected national
stockists.

The four acres of vineyard planted by
Richard Balfour-Lyon in 2002 at Hush
Heath comprise part of a wider 400-acre
estate that includes apple orchards, lake,
formal garden and an ancient woodland, all
belonging to the Tudor manor house.

The vineyard was planted in pursuit of
the finest rosé sparkling wine, an ambition
aided by the site's south-facing aspect and
gentle slope. The owner's dream has been
realised with the acquisition of several
regional, national and international awards
and medals; and the vineyard's esteemed
rosé has been served to first-class flyers
with British Airways and passengers aboard
the Orient Express.

All the sparkling wines at Hush Heath are
made from the classic champagne grapes in
the vineyard's own winery, and the vineyard
has also recently opened an enlarged
visitor facility for tastings and sales.

When the harvest allows, good still wines
are also produced at Hush Heath, in
addition to sparkling cider from the apple
orchards.

WHITE

(1) Cuvée Skye – 2014
12.0% – (11.0 g/lt)
Brut
*Citrus fruit and brioche notes with slight salt
and steely lime acidity*
Chardonnay (100%)

(2) 1503 Classic Cuvée – NV
11.5% – (15.7 g/lt)
Extra Sec
*Apple and dried herbs with white pepper
and lemony acidity*
Pinot Noir, Chardonnay, Pinot Meunier

(2) Leslie's Reserve – NV
11.5% – (19.0 g/lt)
Extra Sec
*Brioche and red apple with lime, redcurrant
and fresh acidity*
Pinot Noir, Chardonnay, Pinot Meunier

Blanc de Blancs – 2014
12.0% – (4.0 g/lt)
Brut
*White pepper and herbs with citrus and
steely lime*
Chardonnay (100%)

ROSÉ

** (2) Balfour Brut Rosé – 2014
12.0% – (10.7 g/lt)
*Rosehip, greengage and apple with white
currant, quince and Lime*
Chardonnay (48%), Pinot Noir (39%),
Pinot Meunier (13%)

1503 Rosé – NV
11.5% – (18.6 g/lt)
Sec
*Citrus and wild strawberries with red berries
and pink grapefruit*
Pinot Noir, Chardonnay, Pinot Meunier

RED

1503 – NV
11.5%
*Strawberry, raspberry and cherry with earthy
notes and balanced acidity*
Pinot Noir

TERLINGHAM

Terlingham Lane, Folkestone, CT18 7AE
01303 892452
terlinghamvineyard.co.uk

4 acres (approx. 1375 vines/acre)
First planted in 2006
Total wine production: 2000 to 5000
bottles annually
Winemaker: Kobus Louw

Terroir
Approx. 160m above sea level
South-facing slope
Chalky soils

Visiting and buying
Easter to Sept, Sat, Sun and bank holidays
by appointment; other times by appointment
only; groups by prior arrangement only; guided
walks and wine tastings by appointment,
March to Sept. Wine sales at cellar door
and online.

The vineyard at Terlingham, planted in 2006,
is part of an estate that dates from the
thirteenth century. Lying on the southern
fringe of the North Downs, with views out
across the English Channel to the French
coast, this family-run boutique vineyard
has used natural farming and winemaking
processes exclusively since 2015.

The sparkling wines are produced in the
onsite winery using the classic champagne
grape varieties. Terlingham also makes
white, rosé and red still wines.

WHITE

Sparkling White – 2012
12.5% – (6.0 g/lt)
Brut
Soft aromas of freshly cut grass and
elderflower, crisp on the palate, flavours
of white and yellow flowers, peaches and
nectarines blend together with biscuitiness
Pinot Noir (55%), Chardonnay (35%),
Pinot Meunier (10%)

ROSÉ

Sparkling Rosé – 2012
12.5% – (8.0 g/lt)
Brut
Berries, pomegranate and orange peel in the
aroma and flavour, a sweet candied quality
with raspberry and blueberry flavours, with
crisp finish
Chardonnay (55%), Pinot Noir (35%),
Pinot Meunier (10%)

ELHAM VALLEY

Breach, Barham, CT4 6LN
01227 831266
elhamvalleyvineyard.com

1.75 acres (approx. 1200 vines/acre)
First planted in 1980
Total wine production: approx. 2000
bottles annually
Winemaker: Charles Simpson

Terroir
Approx. 64m above sea level
South-east facing
Predominantly chalky and flinty soils

Visiting and buying
Open all year, Mon to Sat, 9am to 5pm, Sun,
10am to 4pm; groups by prior arrangement
only. Garden centre and artisan craft
workshops. Wine sales at cellar door and
selected local stockists.

The management of this vineyard is unique
in the UK. Set within the Kent Downs
AONB, Elham Valley is run and managed
by the Fifth Trust charity as a day-education
centre for adults with learning difficulties.
Although small, it is an active, productive
vineyard, growing a number of different
grape varieties.

The sparkling wine, made from non-
champagne grapes, is vinified and stored at
the nearby Simpsons Wine Estate, and then
sold in the Elham Valley shop in aid of the
charity. The vineyard also produces its own
still wine.

WHITE

Quality – 2015/16
12.5%
Brut
Pinot Noir (100%)

Sparkling – 2015/16
12.5%
Brut
Seyval Blanc (100%)

ROSÉ

Sparkling Rosé – 2015/16
12.5%
Brut
Pinot Noir (100%)

ALBURY ORGANIC

Silent Pool, Shere Road, Albury, Surrey,
GU5 9BW
01483 229159
alburyvineyard.com

13 acres (approx. 1600 vines/acre)
First planted in 2009
Total wine production: approx. 20,000
bottles annually
Winemaker: Matthieu Elzinga

Terroir
Approx. 100m above sea level
South-facing slope
Clay soils on chalk

Visiting and buying
Open all year, Sat, 11am to 4pm; by
appointment at other times; groups by prior
arrangement only; self-guided walkabout
when open; guided tours by appointment.
Wine sales at cellar door and selected
stockists.

Nick Wenman hankered after a vineyard
for many years. In 2006, he left a career
in IT and, with his wife and family, found
a site in the Surrey Hills, on the Duke of
Northumberland's estate. Three years later
he planted vines on a plot thought to have
been first cultivated around 1670. The
vineyard was to be farmed organically and
the recognised champagne grape varieties
grown with one exception. Albury's first
vintage, a still rosé, was served on the
Royal Barge during HM Queen Elizabeth II's
Diamond Jubilee in 2012.

The sparkling wines at Albury, now
produced with champagne and non-
champagne grapes, have already become
international award winners.

Albury also produces a Biodynamic Wild
Fermented Blanc de Blancs. This small-batch
sparkling wine, of Chardonnay grapes, is
unusual in that a proportion of the grapes
are hand pressed to preserve the natural
yeasts to be used in the fermentation.

The vineyard also has a brandy distillery
and produces its own honey.

WHITE

(2) Estate Classic Cuvée – 2016
11.5% – (10.5 g/lt)
Brut
Red berries, light citrus and peach with ripe
acidity and subtle sweetness
Pinot Noir (42.5%), Chardonnay (29%),
Pinot Meunier (28.5%)

(1) Blanc de Blancs – 2016
12.0% – (10.8 g/lt)
Brut
Pears, apples and garden herbs with floral
gooseberry
Chardonnay (51%), Seyval Blanc (49%)

ROSÉ

(1) Sparkling Rosé – 2015
12.5% – (4.6 g/lt)
Brut
Red berries and light citrus
Pinot Noir (53%), Pinot Meunier (47%)

DENBIES WINE ESTATE

London Road, Dorking, RH5 6AA
01306 876616
denbies.co.uk

265 acres (approx. 1150 vines/acre)
First planted in 1986
Total wine production: around 450,000
bottles annually
Winemakers: John Worontschak
and Matthieu Elzinga

Terroir
Between 50m and 100m above sea level
East and south-facing slopes
Fertile flinty loam overlying chalk

Visiting and buying
April to Dec, Mon to Sat, 9.30am to 5.30pm,
Sun, 10am to 5.30pm; Jan to March, Mon
to Fri, 9.30am to 5pm, Sat, 9.30am to
5.30pm, Sun 10am to 5.30pm; groups by
prior arrangement only; self-guided walkabout
when open; guided tours all year, daily, hourly.
B&B at vineyard. Wine sales at cellar door,
online and at selected local and national
stockists.

Denbies is currently the largest single-site wine-producing vineyard in the UK. It was planted by a local industrialist on specialist advice. The estate on which the vines now grow had originally been purchased as an intensive cattle and pig-rearing enterprise, but the strictures of EU regulations convinced the owners to try an alternative undertaking. The soil and topographical advantages of this area of the South Downs encouraged the planting of a vineyard. Indeed, the area was known for its wine production as far back as Roman times, and was later referenced for its winemaking in literature of the early eighteenth century. The current Denbies vines were duly planted over a seven-year period, beginning in the 1980s.

All of the sparkling wines are produced in the vineyard winery, and are made from both champagne and non-champagne grapes. Over the years, they have been awarded many regional, national and international medals and trophies.

Denbies is an extremely well organised vineyard, and very accommodating to visitors. The guided tour of the vineyard is made by a Land Rover-hauled viewing train and the winery tour by 'people mover'. There is also a well-marked walk around the vineyard for those who want a serious up-and-downhill hike.

Denbies also produces many white, rosé and red still wines and dessert wines.

WHITE

(1) Whitedowns Cuvée – NV
12.0% – (9.2 g/lt)
Dry
*Citrus aromas and hints of brioche with crisp
and refreshing palate*
Seyval Blanc, Reichensteiner

** (2) Greenfields – NV
12.0% – (9.3 g/lt)
Dry
*Yeast and stone fruit aromas and toasty
with fresh citrus flavours*
Pinot Noir, Pinot Meunier, Chardonnay

Cubitt Reserve Blanc de Blancs – 2013
12.5% – (1.0 g/lt)
Extra Brut
*Green apple, citrus and white fruit with
vanilla and minerality*
Chardonnay (100%)

Cubitt Reserve Blanc de Noirs – 2013
11.5% – (4.2 g/lt)
Brut
*Baked pear and rose petal with strawberry
and minerality*
Pinot Noir (100%)

(4) Demi-Sec – NV
12.0% – (48.0 g/lt)
*Brioche and pear aromas with honeysuckle
and sweet apple finish*
Pinot Noir, Pinot Meunier, Chardonnay

ROSÉ

** (1) Whitedowns Rosé – NV
12.0% – (7.2 g/lt)
Dry
*Red berry aromas with multi-layered cherry
palate*
Seyval Blanc, Rondo

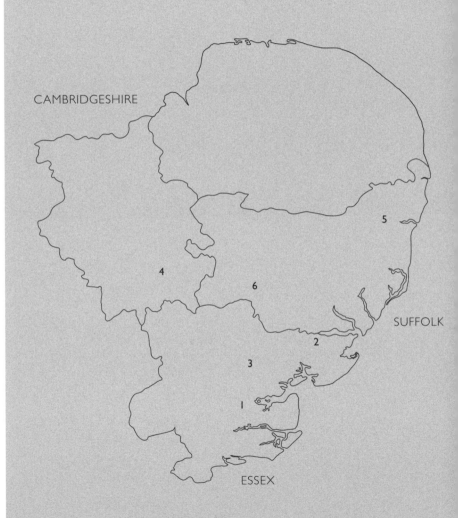

CAMBRIDGESHIRE

SUFFOLK

ESSEX

4

6

5

2

3

1

4. EAST ANGLIA

ESSEX

1. New Hall
2. Dedham Vale
3. West Street

CAMBRIDGESHIRE

4. Chilford Hall

SUFFOLK

5. Valley Farm
6. Giffords Hall

NEW HALL

Chelmsford Road, Purleigh, CM3 6PN
01621 828343
newhallwines.co.uk

106 acres (approx. 1000 vines/acre)
First planted in 1969
Total wine production: approx. 130,000
bottles annually
Winemaker: Rastilav Miklos

Terroir
Between 12m and 24m above sea level
South-facing slopes
Fairly heavy London Clay soil

Visiting and buying
May to Sept, Mon to Fri, 9am to 4pm,
Sat, 10am to 2pm, bank holidays by
appointment only; groups by prior
arrangement only; guided tours, May
to Aug, selected days, 11am. Food and
wine festival, first week of Sept. Wine
sales at cellar door and online.

Bob and Shelia Greenwood planted a vineyard at New Hall in 1969, in an area of the UK first mentioned for its vines in the Domesday Book. With southerly facing slopes and the shelter of the Crouch Valley, it has since become one of the largest single-site vineyards in the country, and was the first British vineyard to produce sparkling wine using the 'traditional method'.

The vineyard remains in the Greenwood family; Bob and Sheila's son, Piers, was named UK Winemaker of the Year on three occasions, before retiring in 2015, whilst the sparkling wines have won several regional, national and international medals and awards.

New Hall's current crop of sparkling wines are all blended from champagne grapes. The vineyard also produces white, rosé and red still wines.

WHITE

* Classical Brut – 2016
12.5% – (5.0 g/lt)
Full bod.
Fresh and fruity with ripe peachy undertones and soft apple
Pinot Noir (70%), Acolon (30%)

ROSÉ

* Pink Brut – 2016
12.5% – (4.0 g/lt)
Red berries and yeastiness with ripe fruit and slight creaminess
Pinot Noir, Acolon, Pinot Blanc

DEDHAM VALE

Green Lane, Boxted, CO4 5TS
01206 271136
dedhamvalevineyard.com

20 acres (approx. 1000 vines/acre)
First planted in 1990
Total wine production: 20,000 to 25,000
bottles annually
Winemakers: Rob Capp and Mark Barnes

Terroir
Between 40m and 43m above sea level
South-facing slope
Sandy loam and gravel soil

Visiting and buying
Good Friday to Dec, Weds to Sun, 12noon
to 5pm; other times by appointment only;
groups by prior arrangement only; self-guided
walkabout (when open); guided tours by
appointment. Wine sales at cellar door,
online and at local stockists.

In 1990, Mary Mudd, an early English
stalwart of UK vineyards, planted a unique
vineyard of 1.5 acres in this Area of
Outstanding Natural Beauty on the edge
of the Stour Valley and Essex Way. It has,
over time, gradually been extended to its
present size. In the beginning, there was
no mains power supply and a reed bed
took care of any waste; wind and biomass
generators contributed to the energy
requirements. The present vineyard forms
part of an estate with lakes and pastures
that can be enjoyed during the well
signposted self-guided tour.

Champagne and non-champagne grapes
are blended for the sparkling wines in the
Dedham Vale winery. White, rosé and red
still wines, together with cider, are also
produced at the vineyard.

WHITE

English Brut – 2015
12.0% – (6.5 g/lt)
Fresh fruit flavours and yeasty overtones
Orion (80%), Chardonnay (20%)

ROSÉ

English Rosé – 2015
12.0% – (6.5 g/lt)
Brut
Crisp and refreshing with strawberry aromas
Orion (70%), Chardonnay (20%),
Pinot Noir (10%)

WEST STREET

West Street Wine Barn, West Street,
Coggeshall, CO6 1NS
01376 563303
weststreetvineyard.co.uk

4.5 acres (approx. 850 vines/acre)
First planted in 1983
Total wine production: approx. 3500
bottles annually
Winemaker: Rastilav Miklos

Terroir
Approx. 22m above sea level
Southerly aspect
Clay with alluvial gravel soils

Visiting and buying
*April to Sept, Sun to Thurs, 9am to 5pm, Fri
and Sat, 9am to 11pm; Oct to March, Sun,
Weds and Thurs, 9am to 5pm, Fri and Sat,
9am to 11pm; wine school; restaurant.*
Wine sales at cellar door.

When the Mohans bought the Coggeshall
vineyard in 2009, the existing 900 vines,
planted some thirty years earlier, were in
need of tender loving care and attention.
That being done, a further 3000 vines
were planted in 2011. By 2012, the new
winery had been built, enabling the
vineyard's grapes to be processed onsite.
The vineyard also boasts an award-winning
restaurant.

The sparkling wines at West Street, made
from the classic champagne grapes, have
been award winners at regional, national
and international level. White and rosé still
wines are also produced at the vineyard.

WHITE

**** Sparkling Wine – 2013**
12.5% – (10.0 g/lt)
Brut
Apple fruit aromas, light and refreshing
Pinot Noir (50%), Chardonnay (50%)

ROSÉ

Sparkling Rosé – 2013
12.5% – (10.0 g/lt)
Brut
Strawberries and cream on the nose
Chardonnay (50%), Pinot Noir (50%)

CHILFORD HALL

Balsham Road, Linton, CB21 4LE
01223 895600
chilfordhall.co.uk

18 acres (approx. 1000 vines/acre)
First planted in 1972
Total wine production: approx. 18,000
bottles annually
Winemaker: Mark Barnes

Terroir
Between 65m and 75m above sea level
South-west facing slopes
Flinty soil overlaying chalk

Visiting and buying
March to Oct, Thurs to Sun, and bank
holidays, 9.30am to 5.30pm, at other
times by appointment only; groups by
prior arrangement only; guided tours by
appointment, March to Oct, daily, 9.30am
and 1.45pm. Wine sales at cellar door, by
mail order and online.

Chilford Hall, one of the first vineyards in
East Anglia in modern times, planted in
1972, is in the grounds of a nineteenth-
century house. Run by the second
generation of growers, the vineyard lies on
south-western facing slopes in the rolling
countryside just to the south of Cambridge.
A rescued and rebuilt seventeenth-century
barn now serves the vineyard as a fully
equipped modern winery.

The award-winning sparkling wines at
Chilford Hall are a blend of champagne and
non-champagne grapes. White, rosé and red
still wines are also produced at the vineyard.

WHITE

Chilford Hundred Graduate – 2014
12.0 % – (2.8 g/lt)
Brut
Fresh and floral with hints of apple and lime
Müller-Thurgau, Pinot Noir

Chilford Hundred Chancellor – NV
11.0% – (2.8 g/lt)
Brut
Green apple, pear and lemon zest
Pinot Noir

ROSÉ

Chilford Hundred Rosé – NV
12.0% –
Full bod./Brut
Strawberries and citrus with lemon, lime
and cream finish
Müller-Thurgau, Reichensteiner, Dornfelder

VALLEY FARM

Rumburgh Road, Wissett, IP19 0JJ
07867 009967
valleyfarmvineyards.co.uk

8 acres (approx. 375 vines/acre)
First planted in 1987
Total wine production: up to 10,000
bottles annually

Terroir
25-35m above sea level
South-facing slope
Alluvial soils over flint

Visiting and buying
Visitors welcomed at any time, either
by arrangement or spontaneously.
Accommodation available in the form of an
off-grid, eco cabin in the vines. Wine sales
at cellar door and by mail order.

The vineyard at Valley Farm lies in a shallow
valley just a few miles from Suffolk's
Heritage Coast, its vines neatly protected
from the easterly winds by Italian Alder
hedges. In recent years, the vintage vines at
Valley Farm have been renovated by Elaine
Heeler and Vanessa Tucker, who bought
the vineyard in 2014. Four years of serious
pruning has encouraged the production
of fine quality grapes leading, in turn, to
award-winning wines.

The vegan-friendly sparkling cuvée at Valley
Farm is made in partnership with the
Knightor winery in Cornwall. The vineyard
also produces white and rosé still wines.

WHITE

**Sundancer 2015
13%
Brut
Lemon and shortbread
Pinot Gris, Pinot Meunier, Pinot Noir

GIFFORDS HALL

Hartest, Bury St Edmunds, IP29 4EX
01284 830799
giffordshall.co.uk

13 acres
First planted in 1986
Winemaker: Guy Howard

Terroir
South-west facing
Between 85m and 91m above sea level
Sandy loam/clay over chalk soil

Visiting and buying
April to Sept, Tues to Sat, and bank
holidays, 11am to 4pm, Nov and Dec,
Tues to Sun, 11am to 4pm, at other
times by appointment only; groups by
prior arrangement only; guided tours
by appointment, selected dates, 11am.
Wine sales at cellar door and online.

This family-owned vineyard, first planted by John Kemp in the 1980s on some of the highest ground in Suffolk, is situated in the Upper Stour Valley on the banks of an ancient river bed near Long Melford. The winery was established in a converted grain store, where many of the grapes were originally foot trodden in the ancient traditional manner. The present owners, Linda and Guy Howard, bought the vineyard in 2004, and have developed the site and its facilities.

The sparkling wines at Giffords Hall are blended from champagne and non-champagne grapes. The vineyard also produces white, rosé and red still wines and fruit liqueurs.

WHITE

** (1) Classic Cuvée – 2016
11.0%
Oaked/Extra Brut
Hints of pear and hazelnut with biscuit-dry and mineral finish
Pinot Noir, Pinot Blanc

** Brut Reserve – NV
11.0%
Oaked
Soft fruit with red apple and subtle spice
Pinot Noir, Reichensteiner

ROSÉ

** Suffolk Pink – NV
11.0%
Brut
Floral with raspberry, redcurrant notes
Pinot Noir, Madeleine Angevine

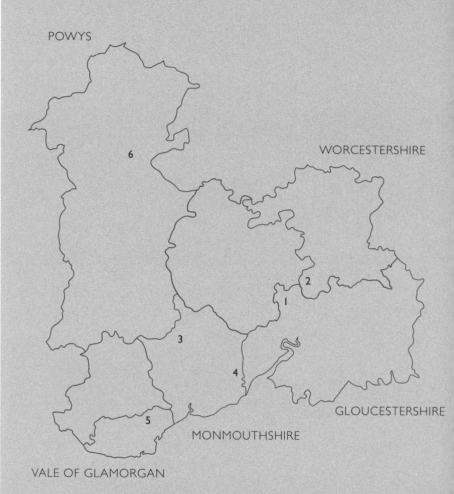

POWYS

WORCESTERSHIRE

6

2

1

3

4

GLOUCESTERSHIRE

5

MONMOUTHSHIRE

VALE OF GLAMORGAN

5. WEST MIDLANDS AND WALES

GLOUCESTERSHIRE
1. Three Choirs

WORCESTERSHIRE
2. Lovells

MONMOUTHSHIRE
3. Sugar Loaf
4. Parva Farm

VALE OF GLAMORGAN
5. Llanerch

POWYS
6. Penarth

THREE CHOIRS

Newent, GL18 1LS
01531 890555
three-choirs-vineyards.co.uk

70 acres (approx. 800 vines/acre)
First planted in 1974
Total wine production: approx. 250,000
bottles annually
Winemaker: Martin Fowke

Terroir
Between 24m and 70m above sea level
Mainly south and south-west facing slopes
Well-drained sandstone

Visiting and buying
Open all year, daily, 9am to 5pm; self-guided
walkabout (when open); guided tour, all year,
Tues to Sun, 2.45pm; mapped walk through
the vines. B&B at vineyard. Wine sales at
cellar door, by mail order and online.

In 1974, Alan McKechnie planted an initial,
experimental half-acre of vines on his
100-acre fruit farm, in the rolling Welsh-
border hills that would give the vineyard
its own particular microclimate. He placed
the vines in unusual widely spaced double
rows. A decade later, Alan sold the vineyard,
and the site has been developed in the
years since; 1991 saw the building of a new
winery and 2000 brought the arrival of
holiday accommodation.

Today, Three Choirs, one of the oldest large
vineyards in the UK, has a national and
international reputation for its own wines
and also for the wines it vinifies for others.
Their own-label sparkling wine is made as
a blend of champagne and non-champagne
grapes. Winemaker Martin Fowke must
be one of the busiest winemakers in the
country; he advises many of the other local
vineyards, who vinify their wines in the
Three Choirs winery. The vineyard also
produces white, rosé and red still wines
and has its own microbrewery.

WHITE

* (2) Classic Cuvée – NV
12.0% – (7.0 g/lt)
Dry
Elegant with elderflower and greengage
flavours
Seyval Blanc, Pinot Noir

LOVELLS

Garrett Bank, Welland, WR13 6NF
01684 311110
lovellsvineyard.co.uk

13 acres (900/1000 vines/acre)
First planted in 2010
Total wine production: approx. 12,000
bottles annually
Winemaker: Martin Fowke (Three Choirs)

Terroir
South-facing slope
Clay and marl soils

Visiting and buying
March to Dec, daily, 11am to 6pm; groups by
prior arrangement only; self-guided walkabout
(when open); guided tour, April to Oct, first Sat
of the month, 11am; arts and crafts centre;
alpacas. Wine sales at cellar door and by
mail order.

Catherine and John Rolinson converted an idea into an actuality in 2010 with the planting of 900 vines. Sitting at the foot of the Malvern Hills in the village of Welland near Upton-upon-Severn, the site they chose has a gentle south-facing slope and particular microclimate. Today, with the ownership and management of three vineyards, the Rolinsons have a total of fifteen acres to tend. Adopting a tradition from one of the vineyards they manage, Catherine and John name their wines after the music of Edward Elgar, who lived in the area.

The cool-climate home-grown non-champagne grapes at Lovells are blended and vinified into sparkling wines at the nearby Three Choirs winery. The vineyard also has its own white and rosé still wines available.

WHITE

Elgar – 2016
12.0% – (2.0 g/lt)
Brut
Citrus notes
Seyval Blanc

ROSÉ

*Ysobel – 2016
12.0% – (2.0 g/lt)
Brut
Complex with yeasty nose
Pinot Noir

SUGAR LOAF

Dunmar Farm, Pentre Lane, Abergavenny,
NP7 7LA
01873 853066
sugarloafvineyard.co.uk

5 acres
First planted in 1992
Winemaker: Martin Fowke (Three Choirs)

Terroir
Between 76m and 96m above sea level
South-facing slopes
Sandy loam soil

Visiting and buying
Easter to Oct, Tues to Fri, 11am to 5.30pm,
Sat, 11am to 6pm, Sun and bank holidays,
11am to 5pm, Nov and Dec, Tues to Sun,
12noon to dusk; self-guided walkabout when
open. Self-catering cottages at vineyard.
Wine sales at cellar door and online.

Louise Ryan and Simon Bloor took
ownership of Sugar Loaf in 2003, breathing
new life into a vineyard first planted in
1992. The vineyard, the only one in the
Brecon Beacons National Park, takes its
name from the Sugar Loaf mountain under
which it lies, enjoying south-facing slopes
and views towards the valley of the River
Usk. High hedges around the vineyard help
to protect the vines from the irregular
inclement weather that can affect the area.

The sparkling wines at Sugar Loaf are
made of non-champagne grapes at the
Three Choirs winery over the border in
Gloucestershire; some have won regional
and national awards and been served at
the Houses of Parliament and at prestige
events. The vineyard also produces its own-
label white and rosé still wines.

WHITE

Hiraeth – 2010
11.0%
Dry
Crisp stone fruit with yeast and good acidity
Seyval Blanc (100%)

ROSÉ

Rhosyn – NV
Crisp and fresh with subtle summer fruit flavours

PARVA FARM

Tintern, Chepstow, NP16 6SQ
01291 689636
parvafarm.com

2.5 acres (approx. 1800 vines/acre)
First planted in 1979
Total wine production: approx. 6000
bottles annually
Winemaker: Martin Fowke (Three Choirs)

Terroir
Between 19m and 40m above sea level
South-facing slope
Sandy loam soils

Visiting and buying
April to Oct, Thurs to Tues, 1pm to 5.30pm,
Nov to March, Thurs to Tues, 11.30am to
4pm; at other times by appointment only; self-
guided tours when open; guided tours, May
to Oct, by appointment. Wine sales at cellar
door and selected local stockists.

On the site of what is believed to have
been a Roman vineyard, and the vineyard
of the monks of Tintern Abbey, the current,
new owners of Parva Farm have revived
an existing planting after years of neglect
and dereliction. The original vineyard was
the first to be planted in Monmouthshire in
modern times. It sits on the steeply sloping
south-facing side of the River Wye valley,
overlooking the ruined abbey.

Both champagne and non-champagne
grapes are used in Parva Farm's sparkling
wines, which are produced for the vineyard
at Three Choirs winery. The wines have
won local, regional and national awards.

Parva Farm also produces white, rosé and
red still wines, siedr (cider) and mead.

WHITE

* Dathliad – 2013
12.0% – (0.5 g/lt)
Extra Brut
Zesty fruit with grapefruit, brioche and long
finish
Seyval Blanc (80%), Huxelrebe (20%)

ROSÉ

Dathliad Rosé – 2010
11.5% – (0.5 g/lt)
Extra Brut
Berry aromas, flavoursome
Pinot Noir (50%), Seyval Blanc (50%)

LLANERCH

Hensol, Pendoylan, CF72 8GG
01443 222716
llanerch-vineyard.co.uk

11 acres
First planted in 1986
**Total wine production: approx. 10,000
bottles annually**
Winemaker: Martin Fowke (Three Choirs)

Terroir
Approx. 50m above sea level
South-facing slope
Sandy loam soils

Visiting and buying
*Open all year, Mon to Sat, 10am to 11pm,
Sun, 12noon to 11pm; at other times by
appointment only; guided tours, April to Oct,
Tues and Weds, 12.30pm and 5pm, Thurs
to Mon, 12.30pm, 3pm and 5pm; cookery
school.* Hotel accommodation at vineyard.
Wine sales at cellar door.

This former dairy farm dating from the
1700s was planted with vines in 1986 by
the then owners Peter and Diana Andrews,
inspired by the historic (and long gone)
example of Cardiff Castle vineyard only a
short distance away. Today, Llanerch is one
of the oldest and larger vineyards in Wales.

Present owner Ryan Davies bought the
vineyard in 2010 after it had laid derelict
for more than two years; he restored and
replanted the vineyard in unusually wide
single and double rows of vines and over
the years has developed the site into a
tourist and hospitality centre.

Llanerch's sparkling wines are produced
from cool-climate non-champagne grapes.
Initially made in the winery that had been
created in the old cow byre of the original
farm, today the wines are produced at the
Three Choirs winery in Gloucestershire.

The vineyard also produces white and rosé
still wines.

WHITE

Cariad Brut – 2016
11.5%
*Bright fruit aromas with fluffy vanilla sugar
sweetness*
Seyval Blanc

ROSÉ

Cariad Blush – 2011
11.5%
Brut
*Strawberry nose with ripe sweet fruit notes
and zesty finish*
Seyval Blanc (95%), Triomphe (5%)

PENARTH

Pool Road, Newtown, SY16 3AN
07933 671495
penarthvineyard.co.uk

9.75 acres (approx. 1000 vines/acre)
First planted in 1999
Winemaker: Martin Fowke (Three Choirs)

Terroir
West-facing slopes

Visiting and buying
Easter to Dec, daily, 12noon to 4pm; groups
by prior arrangement only; self-guided tours
by appointment. Wine sales at cellar door
and online.

Penarth vineyard, situated at Newtown,
mid-Wales, enjoys a unique microclimate
in the sheltered valley of the River
Severn. Temperatures here can fluctuate
by as much as five degrees Celsius
within a distance of just 500 metres. The
moderating effects of the Gulf Stream
here duly allow for the growing of the
recognised champagne grapes, which are
made into wine at the Three Choirs winery.

The vineyard also has a brandy distillery
and has its own label of white still wines
and brandy available for sale.

WHITE

Blanc de Blancs – NV
Dry/Aromatic
Crisp/gooseberry finish
Chardonnay

ROSÉ

Pink Sparkling – 2006
Fruity/harmonious tannins
Pinot Noir, Pinot Meunier

5

DERBYSHIRE

3

2

1

4

STAFFORDSHIRE

SHROPSHIRE

6. NORTH

SHROPSHIRE
1. Kerry Vale
2. Wroxeter Roman

DERBYSHIRE
3. Renishaw Hall

STAFFORDSHIRE
4. Halfpenny Green

WEST YORKSHIRE
5. Leventhorpe

KERRY VALE

Pentreheyling, SY15 6HU
01588 620627
kerryvalevineyard.co.uk

5.5 acres (approx. 1100 vines/acre)
First planted in 2010
Total wine production: approx. 8000
bottles annually
Winemaker: Clive Vickers

Terroir
Approx. 146m above sea level
Easterly aspect
Stony and well-drained soil

Visiting and buying
June to Oct, Weds to Sun, 10am to 4pm,
Nov and Dec, Weds to Sun, 10am to
3pm; groups by prior arrangement only;
guided tours by appointment, April to
Nov, Thurs, Sat and Sun. Wine sales
at cellar door, online and at selected
local stockists.

In 2010, a year after Geoff and June Ferguson bought an old blacksmith's house, complete with several dilapidated outbuildings, they decided (over a few glasses) to plant vines. Their chosen site lies less than a mile from the Welsh border, where once stood Pentreheyling, a Roman fort, which may itself have been predated by a Bronze Age settlement.

During its short life, the family-run vineyard, now in its second generation, has won many regional, national and international awards for its wines. Development of the site continues, most recently with the addition of a new visitor centre.

The vineyard's sparkling wines are made at the Halfpenny Green vineyard from non-champagne grapes. Kerry Vale also produces its own white, rosé and red still wines.

WHITE

Sparkling White – 2016
12.0% – (10.0 g/lt)
Light bod./Brut
Toasty notes
Phoenix (100%)

ROSÉ

Sparkling Rosé – 2014
12.0% – (12.0 g/lt)
Light bod./Brut
Soft red fruits and elegant finish
Phoenix (96%), Rondo (4%)

RED

Sparkling Red – 2016
12.0% – (12.0 g/lt)
Brut
Dark forest fruit
Rondo (100%)

WROXETER ROMAN

Glebe Farm, Wroxeter, SY5 6PQ
01743 761888
wroxetervineyard.co.uk

9 acres
First planted in 1991
Winemaker: Martin Millington

Terroir
Approx. 55m above sea level
South and south-west facing
Light sandy soil

Visiting and buying
Open all year, Mon to Sat, 9am to 5pm,
Sun, 10.30am to 4.30pm; groups by prior
arrangement only; guided tours, Easter to
Oct, Sat and Sun, 10.30am. Camping and
accommodation at vineyard. Wine sales at
cellar door and online.

Viroconium Cornoviorum (now the village
of Wroxeter) is thought to have been
the fourth largest town in Roman Britain.
And it seems likely that Wroxeter Roman,
planted on an existing farm, has taken root
on the site of a Roman vineyard. Sheltered
by the Cambrian mountains, the vineyard
benefits from over a thousand hours of
sunshine annually, encouraging earlier
ripening grapes to give the resultant wines
a sweeter taste.

The sparkling wine at Wroxeter Roman
is made at the Three Choirs winery from
non-champagne grapes. The vineyard
produces white, rosé and red still wines in
its own onsite winery.

WHITE

Vintage Reserve
Med. bod./Brut
Fragrant apple aroma with refreshing acidity
Reichensteiner, Madeleine Angevine

RENISHAW HALL

Eckington, S21 3WB
01246 432310
renishaw-hall.co.uk

1.25 acres
First planted in 1972
Total wine production: approx. 2000
bottles annually
Winemaker: Kieron Atkinson

Terroir
Approx. 79m above sea level
Sandy loam soil

Visiting and buying
April to Sept, Weds to Sun and bank
holidays, 10.30am to 4.30pm, Oct and
Nov, Fri and Sat, 10.30am to 4pm; groups
by prior arrangement only; guided tours by
appointment, April to Sept, selected Sundays.
Wine sales at visitor centre, by mail order,
online and at selected local and national
stockists.

The vineyard at Renishaw Hall is situated
in the old walled kitchen garden, some
way away from the award-winning formal
gardens on the Sitwell family estate.
The wall that surrounds the vineyard on
three sides has a radiating effect on the
vines, raising the average temperature by
approximately one degree celsius. Planted
by Sir Sacheverell Reresby Sitwell in 1972,
at the time the vineyard was believed
to be the most northerly in the world
(today's most northerly is thought to be
in Norway). Renishaw Hall has a singular
microclimate, shaped by the protection
of the surrounding hills. Even so, the
sparkling wines here are produced from
non-champagne cool-climate grapes at
Halfpenny Green Winery.

Renishaw Hall also sells its own white, rosé
and red still wines.

WHITE

White Sparkling – 2014
11.5%
Lemon zest and brioche with rich biscuit,
citrus hints and firm acidity
Seyval Blanc (100%)

ROSÉ

Rosé Sparkling – 2014
12%
Brut
Rhubarb, strawberry, raspberry, red apple
and brioche
Seyval Blanc (90%), Rondo (10%)

HALFPENNY GREEN

Tom Lane, Halfpenny Green, Bobbington,
DY7 5EP
01384 221122
halfpenny-green-vineyards.co.uk

30 acres (approx. 1300 vines/acre)
First planted in 1983
Total wine production: 200,000 to
250,000 bottles annually
Winemaker: Ben Hunt

Terroir
Between 67m and 70m above sea level
South to south-west facing slopes
Light sandy free-draining soils

Visiting and buying
*Open all year, daily, 9.30am to 5pm;
groups by prior arrangement only;
guided tours by appointment, selected
dates, 12noon or 6.30pm; craft centre,
fishing and the Wild Zoological Park.
Wine sales at cellar door, online and
at farmers' markets.*

In 1983, Martin Vickers planted half an acre of vines on the farm that had been in his family since the 1930s. Initially, he was a hobby grower, but in 1990 he expanded the area under vine to twenty acres. Unusually, the vines at Halfpenny Green are planted facing east/west, as well as the usual south facing. Today, the vineyard has grown further, to thirty acres, and provides the main focus for the family farm, overseen by Martin's son, Clive.

The guided tour at Halfpenny Green concludes in a 300-year-old oak barn for the wine tasting. The recently expanded winery serves some sixty other growers from the surrounding area, thirty of whom produce sparkling wine, and features ninety-two storage tanks, to cope with the demand. The estate owners pride themselves in having a boutique vineyard, even while it has grown to become one of the larger vineyards in the UK.

The own-label sparkling wines at Halfpenny Green, made both from champagne and non-champagne grapes, have won many regional, national and international awards and medals and have been used at several regal and governmental events.

The vineyard also produces many white, rosé and red own-label still wines.

WHITE

Brut Sparkling – 2016
11.5% – (10.0 g/lt)
Seyval Blanc (70%), Pinot Noir (20%), Chardonnay (10%)

Classic Cuvée – 2011
11.5% – (9.0 g/lt)
Brut
Crunchy red berries
Pinot Noir (70%), Chardonnay (30%)

(1) White Sparkling – 2014
12.0%
Brut
Light citrus character, nutty and balanced
Seyval Blanc, Pinot Noir, Chardonnay

ROSÉ

Rosé Sparkling – 2016
11.5% – (9.0 g/lt)
Light bod./Dry
Pinot Noir (70%), Seyval Blanc (30%)

LEVENTHORPE

Bullerthorpe Lane, Woodlesford, Leeds,
LS26 8AF
0113 2889088
leventhorpevineyard.co.uk

5 acres (approx. 1650 vines/acre)
First planted in 1986
Winemaker: George Bowden

Terroir
Between 18m and 26m above sea level
South-facing gentle slope
Sandy loam overlying sand and broken
sandstone

Visiting and buying
*Open all year (calling ahead is
recommended), Mon to Sat, 11am to
4pm, Sun, 12noon to 4pm; groups by
prior arrangement only.* Wine sales at
cellar door and by mail order.

When George Bowden planted his vineyard a short distance to the east of Leeds in 1986, he took the latitude of viticulture in the UK to new northerly extremes (extremes that have subsequently been surpassed by other vineyards). The slope and orientation of the site give the vineyard its own particular, beneficial microclimate. The wines at Leventhorpe are made from grapes that have a shorter ripening season but a significantly longer maturation period than most. This longer maturation, together with the selection of grape varieties, produces sparkling wines that are considerably different on the palate.

The medal-winning sparkling wines at Leventhorpe are produced in the vineyard's winery from non-champagne grapes. Both white and red still wines are also produced at the vineyard.

WHITE

(1) Yorkshire Brut – 2013
12.0% – (1.0 g/lt)
Brioche and bready with citrus, green apple and softly honeyed
Seyval Blanc (100%)

ROSÉ

(1) Rosé Gold – 2013
12.0% – (1.0 g/lt)
Brut
Light and refreshing
Seyval Blanc (85%), Pinot Noir (15%)

ISBN: 9781851499052

British Library Cataloguing-in-Publication Data
A catalogue record for this book is available from the British Library

The author and publisher gratefully acknowledge the permission granted to reproduce the copyright material in this book. Every effort has been made to trace copyright holders and to obtain their permission for the use of copyright material. The publisher apologises for any errors or omissions in the text and would be grateful if notified of any corrections that should be incorporated in future reprints or editions of this book.

With thanks to Gill, my perpetual mentor; Roger, my early mentor; and Trudy, my latter mentor.

Editor: Andrew Whittaker
Designer: Craig Holden
Picture Researcher: Bryn Porter

Front cover image: © Camel Valley Wines 2018
Back cover image: © Courtesy of Nyetimber Vineyard

Printed in China
for ACC Art Books Ltd, Woodbridge, Suffolk, England

www.accartbooks.com